Organize
Your
Stuff

The Lazy Way™

Organize Your Stuff

Toni Ahlgren

The Lazy Way™

Macmillan • USA

To my beautiful boys Niklas, Douglas and Thomas, who saw a little less of me one summer while I worked this. This is for you guys with all my love.

T.A.

Macmillan Publishing books may be purchased for business or sales promotional use. For information please write: Special Markets Department, Macmillan Publishing USA, 1633 Broadway, New York, NY 10019-6785.

International Standard Book Number: 0-02-863000-9
Library of Congress Catalog Card Number: 98-89983

01 00 99   8 7 6 5 4 3 2 1

Interpretation of the printing code: the rightmost number of the first series of numbers is the year of the book's printing; the rightmost number of the second series of numbers is the number of the book's printing. For example, a printing code of 99-1 shows that the first printing occurred in 1999.

Printed in the United States of America

Book Design: Madhouse Studios

Page creation by Carrie Allen, Heather Pope, and Trina Wurst.

You Don't Have to Feel Guilty Anymore!

IT'S O.K. TO DO IT *THE LAZY WAY!*

It seems every time we turn around, we're given more responsibility, more information to absorb, more places we need to go, and more numbers, dates, and names to remember. Both our bodies and our minds are already on overload. And we know what happens next—cleaning the house, balancing the checkbook, and cooking dinner get put off until "tomorrow" and eventually fall by the wayside.

So let's be frank—we're all starting to feel a bit guilty about the dirty laundry, stacks of ATM slips, and Chinese take-out. Just thinking about tackling those terrible tasks makes you exhausted, right? If only there were an easy, effortless way to get this stuff done! (And done right!)

There is—*The Lazy Way*! By providing the pain-free way to do something—including tons of shortcuts and time-saving tips, as well as lists of all the stuff you'll ever need to get it done efficiently—*The Lazy Way* series cuts through all of the time-wasting thought processes and laborious exercises. You'll discover the secrets of those who have figured out *The Lazy Way*. You'll get things done in half the time it takes the average person—and then you will sit back and smugly consider those poor suckers who haven't discovered *The Lazy Way* yet. With *The Lazy Way,* you'll learn how to put in minimal effort and get maximum results so you can devote your attention and energy to the pleasures in life!

THE LAZY WAY PROMISE

Everyone on *The Lazy Way* staff promises that, if you adopt *The Lazy Way* philosophy, you'll never break a sweat, you'll barely lift a finger, you won't put strain on your brain, and you'll have plenty of time to put up your feet. We guarantee you will find that these activities are no longer hardships, since you're doing them *The Lazy Way*. We also firmly support taking breaks and encourage rewarding yourself (we even offer our suggestions in each book!). With *The Lazy Way*, the only thing you'll be overwhelmed by is all of your newfound free time!

THE LAZY WAY SPECIAL FEATURES

Every book in our series features the following sidebars in the margins, all designed to save you time and aggravation down the road.

- **"Quick 'n' Painless"**—shortcuts that get the job done fast.
- **"You'll Thank Yourself Later"**—advice that saves time down the road.
- **"A Complete Waste of Time"**—warnings that spare countless headaches and squandered hours.
- **"If You're So Inclined"**—optional tips for moments of inspired added effort.
- **"The Lazy Way"**—rewards to make the task more pleasurable.

If you've either decided to give up altogether or have taken a strong interest in the subject, you'll find information on hiring outside help with "How to Get Someone Else to Do It" as well as further reading recommendations in "If You Really Want More, Read These." In addition, there's an only-what-you-need-to-know glossary of terms and product names ("If You Don't Know Where to Get It, Look Here") as well as "It's Time for Your Reward"—fun and relaxing ways to treat yourself for a job well done.

With *The Lazy Way* series, you'll find that getting the job done has never been so painless!

Series Editor
Amy Gordon

Editorial Director
Gary Krebs

Director of Creative Services
Michele Laseau

Cover Designer
Michael Freeland

Managing Editor
Robert Shuman

Development Editor
Alana Morgan

Production Editor
Kristi Hart

What's in This Book

Part 3   **The Room-by-Room Treatment Plan**   **57**

It's Time to Take Control of Your Stuff, and Here's How to Do It!

Life is complicated. I don't know about you, but it seems to me that it's getting more complicated with each passing moment. In spite of all the technology and labor-saving devices out there, most of us still feel as if we're just one step ahead of the eight ball—and are sometimes crushed by it when our systems fail.

I'm going to make the wild assumption that you'd rather take a bike ride than spend 3 hours paying your bills, that you'd rather sit in the sandbox with your children than look for a lost library book, or that you'd love to have another hour at work instead of visiting the grocery store for the fourth time in a week. Time is one of our most precious resources, and how we allocate our time is key to managing our lives.

How, then, do we manage to get more in control of our time and stuff? There are ways and systems you can adopt to make your life run more like a well-oiled machine. There will always be screw-ups, of course, humans being what they are, but you can set things in motion—*The Lazy Way*—to minimize routine chores and maximize your free time.

A lot of this book covers paper because, if you're like most people, you are drowning in a sea of paper of every sort. Receipts, your children's artwork, junk mail, little scraps of paper with pertinent phone numbers. . . all this paper is frequently cited as the most overwhelming organizational problem people face today. It comes by Pony Express, Federal Express, and the mail carrier, and is produced by newspaper and magazine publishers, the credit card companies, and secret high-speed presses with machines that slap on labels with your name and address. In this book I will show you how to not spend one more second than absolutely necessary on managing all that paper.

I hope you find several ideas you can apply to your life for quick results. You will sometimes find more than one way to do something in this book. That's because we all have different learning styles and different tolerances for disorder or clutter, or you may even have a workable system already established that could use some fine-tuning. Pick out the parts you can use immediately, and go to it.

Be good to yourself. Getting organized is an ongoing process and can't be done overnight. What's more, our lives change, so our needs change. Children come and children go, for example, requiring vastly different approaches to keep all systems functioning well. Sometimes we have money, and sometimes we don't. Either circumstance affects how much help we can hire to do some of the organizing for us. Like everything else in life, the only thing you can count on is change, and this means your organizing systems will need continuous tweaking to accommodate your life.

A word about stuff: Less is more. What it costs to own things is enormous in the time spent acquiring it, the mileage spent exchanging it, the real estate required to store it, the outlay to clean, repair, and update it, the stress of losing it, and the agony of ruining it.

Here are some thoughts that might be new to you. Try to apply them and you will keep organizing agony to a minimum:

- Try to think "needs" versus "wants."
- What you acquire should be the best and most versatile you can afford.
- There are very few things that can't be replaced, so let them go.
- Evaluate everything you own: Does it do something useful?
- Other people often need your stuff more than you do.

Think about the disorganized areas in your life causing you the most distress. Start there, if you like, and follow the suggestions in this book. Slowly but surely, you can tackle each chapter and make the changes in your life that make sense to you. And don't aim for perfection. Set your sights on a fairly smoothly functioning home or office and on spending as little time as possible looking for lost stuff.

Remember, it's no more painful or time-consuming to be organized than it is to be disorganized. So let's get started!

Thank You...

This has been a relatively short, intense and delightful gestation period and I'm proud to share what I know about organizing.

My thanks to the professionals: my agent, Martha Casselman, who asked the question; Editor Amy Gordon for trusting I'd come through; Alana Morgan, who enthusiastically encouraged me all the way; buddies Julie Ann Kodmur who streamlined and Karen Miller for the cute stuff; all my clients who taught me so much about the need for order, simplicity, and efficiency.

And to Connie Cox, who called me a professional organizer before I even knew I was one and with whom I can spend many rapturous hours in an office supply store.

If everybody who reads this book can be inspired to make just one change to improve the quality of their lives, I will consider my efforts worthwhile.

T.A.

Stuff, Stuff, and More Stuff, But Just the Right Stuff

Are you too lazy to read Stuff, Stuff, and More Stuff, but Just the Right Stuff?

1 Was the last time you used a binder in high school?
☐ yes ☐ no

2 You can't hang your clothes up—the closets won't hold any more.
☐ yes ☐ no

3 The last time you saw the garden rake was when you brought it home from the store last Spring. ☐ yes ☐ no

Tools for Making Your Life Tidier

You wouldn't ask a plumber to do his job without the right tools, right? You, too, need some basic supplies to make fast work of getting yourself organized. Have these on hand to make your work sessions flow!

YOUR OFFICE

Here are a few of the basic supplies you need to get your office—be it a nook somewhere or a whole room—in perfect working order. Chapter 6, "Getting the Home Office Up to Speed," will give you more ideas and how to best use these supplies.

- Desk
- Work chair
- File cabinets (the best you can afford)
- Hanging folders
- Manila folders (letter or legal; third cut, which means the tabs are big enough to write boldly in large letters)

- Folder holders (such as Eldon's Add-A-File) to prop manila folders upright on your desktop
- Permanent markers for labeling folders
- Stapler, staple remover, and staples
- Good lamp
- Tape
- Removable Scotch tape (in the blue box)
- Paper clips
- Post-It notes in assorted sizes
- Banker's boxes
- Wastepaper basket (size XXL)
- Telephone headset

CLOSETS

Your closet might benefit from a good cleaning out more than anything else, but you could probably use at least a couple of the following items to maximize your space. And don't forget that some of these things lend themselves to use in the linen closet and children's closets.

- Plastic bins
- Closet rod to hang below existing one
- Hooks
- Wire baskets and frames to hold them
- Shoe holders, hangers, or boxes
- Matching hangers, including suit hangers for hanging a top over a clipped skirt or pants
- Shoe trees

KITCHEN

Obviously, you won't be able to use all the handy items listed below. But after you've cleared out your kitchen, you'll find that some of them will really help your organizing efforts.

- Pretty vinyl shelf paper
- Bins for under the sink and in cabinets
- Wire racks for holding plates and/or canned foods
- Turntables for cupboards
- Wire or plastic drawer dividers
- Wine rack
- Hooks
- Pegboard for hanging things
- Cup hooks
- Paper bag holder and plastic organizer to hold boxes of aluminum foil and plastic wrap
- Cardboard or plastic tubes to hold used plastic bags
- Baskets to hold large utensils, soup mixes, or vitamin bottles
- Bulletin board

GARAGE/RECYCLING/LAUNDRY

See Chapter 11, "Conquering the Chaotic Spots," for how to best make use of these tools:

- More plastic bins (am I repeating myself?)
- Hooks to hold anything that can be hung

QUICK  PAINLESS

Use your refrigerator as a valuable storage area. Photographic film, new batteries, and expensive creams can all call the refrigerator their home and will stay fresh longer.

- Hooks made specifically to hang bicycles, skis, and so on
- Steel shelving unit(s)
- Boxes or bins, tool cases, fishing tackle cases, or units made specifically for nuts, bolts, and other hardware
- Round holders to snap in broom or rake handles
- Recycling bins, with compartments for dividing different types of recyclables
- Pegboard on which to hang tools
- Rolling cart
- #17 rubber bands
- Clothesline
- Plastic tubular hangers

KIDS

Some of the following items might be better suited for your playroom or family room than your child's room. And what I've specified might work for toddlers yet be highly inappropriate for teens! Please just use this list as inspiration for your specific situation.

- Bins, buckets, baskets, tubs, and shoe boxes (cardboard or plastic) for toys or toy pieces
- Hooks for eye-level, off-the-floor storage
- Bookcases or shelf units
- Lamps (with an eye on safety)

IF YOU'RE SO
INCLINED

A rectangular shoe organizer with cubbies in it can be a perfect storage solution for small stuffed animals, doll clothes, cars and trucks, and other toys your children consider treasures.

- Low table and a couple of chairs
- Bulletin board or chalkboard
- Toy chest
- A second closet rod
- Duvet covers for beds
- Zip-lock plastic bags for tiny collections
- Egg cartons

BATHROOM

You may have room enough to move an actual piece of furniture into your bathroom. Others will be pleased to find the space to accommodate another roll of toilet paper. Either way, pick and choose from the list below after reading Chapter 13, "Bringing Your Bathroom to Bear."

- Hooks, hooks, and more hooks
- Plastic bins for under-the-sink area or to place on shelves
- Towels and bath mats in same color
- Vinyl shelf paper
- Turntables for cabinet floors
- Baskets
- Stacking plastic boxes
- Zip-lock bags
- Drawer dividers
- Hamper

A COMPLETE WASTE OF TIME

The 3 Worst Things to Have in a Bathroom (and Why):

1. Anything made of glass (poses a safety risk).
2. Toilet tank and seat covers (two more things to get dirty and require laundering).
3. Crocheted toilet-paper roll covers (dust catchers and just plain junky).

Store sleeping bags (as well as blankets and down comforters) by rolling them up and using a bungee cord to hold them tightly rolled. Then slip them into a large plastic bag to keep out moisture and dust.

- Small chest or bench
- Mesh bag to hold kids' toys
- Caddy to hold tubes and bottles in the shower
- Toilet brush in a stand
- Small supply of cleaning products
- Mirrors wherever possible
- Wastepaper basket

BEDROOM

Making and keeping your bedroom a paradise is not such a daunting task if you use some of these tools!

- A duvet cover to replace the top sheet, blanket, and bedspread
- A blanket stand to hold your bedspread (if you use one and take it off at night) or quilts
- Plastic bins for under-the-bed storage
- Hooks for pajamas, robes, sweats, or tomorrow's suit and tie
- Bedside tables (see Chapter 9, "No More Nightmares," to come up with some innovative alternatives to standard tables)
- Baskets for magazines and newspapers
- Good lamps
- Laundry hamper
- Small baskets, covered jars, and pretty bowls to collect clutter

Getting Time on Your Side

	The Old Way	The Lazy Way
Keeping your files in order	2 hours of moving piles around every day	10 minutes, once a day
Finding the other shoe	Consider it lost if it's in the closet!	2 seconds— it's in the shoe organizer!
Getting all your ingredients together to make a meal	1 hour	2 minutes
Extracting the bicycle from the garage	I swear it's in there!	2 seconds!
Finding your child's LEGO™ set	Oh God...there's some here, a few there...	It's all in one box!
Cleaning up the bathroom after the morning rush	An entire day	A few minutes and you're done!

Chapter two

Outfitting to Organize

I t's one of those mysterious truths that to organize the stuff you already have, you need to get yourself some other stuff to help you reach your goal. So here's a list of some of the major organizational tools you need to consider to get yourself organized. You're not going to need all these items, but the following paragraphs are simply here to give you an overview of most of the basics that can be used. Turn to the appendices to find contact numbers and addresses for the equipment I've listed below.

COMPUTERS: YES OR NO?

Computers, obviously, are the way to organize many facets of your life. They are indispensable for word processing, initially, and can simplify keeping track of extraordinary amounts of the information you need for whatever reason, in many different forms. For example, an address book is usually derived from the information you enter in a database program. Once all the information is entered, you can make labels, print out a telephone list, or sort your entries by ZIP code. There are all kinds of ways to play with the same information, and having that ability means you can guarantee that all your stuff is organized in a way that is logical for you, instead of some random software developer.

However, at the risk of sounding highly un-technical and definitely politically incorrect, I must share some doubts that everyone needs a computer. I've come to the conclusion that you must be highly motivated and have a sense of urgency about wanting to use a computer before you should invest in one or learn how to use one. The learning curve is slow, no doubt about it, and unless you have a real need for what the computer can offer you, you may not stick it out during the learning process. I've observed that most people reach a point where they're ready to throw the blasted thing out the window rather than deal with untold amounts of frustration in the learning stages of computerland.

Additionally, I don't believe computers save much time. They enable you to create more and generate more work, but because of the learning time, occasional "crashes," and time spent updating equipment and software, it's a wash time-wise.

If you're not motivated to learn about computers, if you're not sure you need one, or if you haven't tried someone else's computer, you may be better off sticking to your index cards and a typewriter. However, if you decide that you do need one (and most certainly your children need one), then survey your computer-savvy friends, relatives, and work associates. Read everything you can get your hands on to determine approximately what you need in the way of equipment and just how

IF YOU'RE SO INCLINED

Another option, and one that will save you a lot of time, is to enlist the help of a consultant, one who can help you buy, set up, install, and train you on your new toy. See Appendix A, "How to Get Someone Else to Do It," if you need convincing that this is the most efficient way to get started.

you'll use your computer before you even think about going into a store and questioning salespeople.

ELECTRONIC ORGANIZERS

A new breed of helpful tool has been born from the needs of people on the go who can't be in their offices all day every day to manage their information from their desktop computers. "Personal Information Managers" (PIMs), or "Personal Digital Assistants" (PDAs), if you prefer, are pocket-sized dynamos which perform the most amazing tasks. Read more about electronic organizers in Chapter 3, "Tricks of the Trade."

FAX MACHINE

One essential is a fax machine. You might wonder how you'd ever make use of one, but after three months of having one, you'll wonder how you ever got along without one. Be sure to read the section on using a fax machine in Chapter 6, "Getting the Home Office Up to Speed."

COPIER

If you can justify the expense for your home, seriously consider a copier. Canon makes a model that I've seen for under $300, and it will change your life. Just think—no more running to the copy center!

GENERAL ORGANIZATIONAL TOOLS

Organizational tools are now, thankfully, widely available. I'm mentioning several large chains for quick

QUICK ⬭ PAINLESS

An electronic organizer is a fraction of the size of a planner, can hold more information, and does the searching for you—what could be better?!

one-stop shopping convenience, but let me point out that small, local suppliers often offer excellent service and personal interest in solving your organizational dilemmas, if not the cheapest prices. They may not always have the selection you are used to, but I've found that most of them can order what you need and have it available within a few days. Be sure to support these "little guys" if you can.

Having said that, one of your best shopping sources are the large chain stores such as Target, Long's Drugs, WalMart, Office Depot, Staples, and Office Max. Here you will find plastic bins, plastic bags, closet organization accessories, storage carts, shelf units, and furniture.

Shelving

Large home-improvement centers can supply you with many of the products mentioned in this book. Shelving units, or the raw materials to build them, are the most important of these products, since you want to increase your shelf space by about 3,000 percent.

Chain hardware stores carry a blend of the offerings mentioned above. You'll also find lighting solutions, shelving units, ready-made shelves, or raw materials for building them. You'll find selections of hooks and closet fixtures as well.

Office Furniture

Try the chains first for office equipment in a range of prices and quality. (Buy the best you can afford.) Staples, Office Depot, and Office Max are good choices for file cabinets, desks, and real office chairs. Fine furniture stores offer high-style, high-quality office furniture that can be integrated into a formal home or status office.

Office Supplies

Again, the office-supply chains might be your best bet for paper goods, such as folders, desk accessories, and labeling equipment.

In addition to local suppliers, try mail-order suppliers. I use Quill when I'm buying anything in bulk; the quality is good and you can't beat the price or fast delivery. Viking is another good source.

Labeling machines are great and can help in your quest for order. Dymo Labelers, which can emboss or print on plastic strips, seem to have taken a backseat to electronic label machines such as those manufactured by Kroy and Brother. Just about the size of an adding machine, they make high-quality printed labels on different-colored tape in a variety of typefaces and sizes. You can buy them at office-supply stores and through catalogs.

Closet/Storage Builders

If you have the budget, bring in professionals who do nothing except design and build storage solutions. Their designs work in closets, garages, home offices, and places you probably haven't thought of. Be sure to get references and look at their work at customers' homes, rather than just showrooms. Don't get talked into a system that uses special hangers or equipment. Remember, the point

Congratulations! You're beginning to regain control over your house! Now take a break and schedule some play time for yourself. All work and no play is no fun!

The Lazy Way

Not all storage units have to look like storage units. Think of an armoire: It's not just for linens. If one would fit into your space, budget, and decor, think about using it to store your photograph albums, hobby supplies, or collection of rocks. A wooden trunk can serve as both a living room coffee table or an end-of-the-bed item and could hold books, bulky bedspreads, or out-of-season clothes. A window seat adds charm in a room, and if it's constructed so that you can lift the seat, you'll gain extra storage space.

is to simplify. These companies can come up with many solutions to storage problems.

Slide-out drawers, plastic or wire, maximize your space under sinks and in cupboards and drawers. You can find them at the "big box" stores, such as Target, Home Depot, and large hardware stores.

BIG-TICKET ITEMS FOR THE BEDROOM

Beds, of course, are usually the biggest (and most used) item in bedrooms. Make sure you've got maximum comfort, firmness, and support. Then think about an important secondary use of the bed—as a storage option. A high bed can offer a mass of storage space, with no one the wiser if a dust ruffle covers everything up.

Another option that might work for you is a bed on a platform with pull-out drawers underneath, which hold lots of stuff! A way to add a sleeping spot without taking up more space is a trundle bed. The lower bed slides underneath the upper one; they're great in kids' rooms for sleep-overs. If you want to use high space instead of low space, bunk beds are the ticket: two beds in the space of one, or one bed over a desk or play area.

Other bedroom furnishings are storage units to hold clothes, books, and the television or stereo. Generally, I'd advise you not to purchase bedside tables, but use real furniture instead. (See Chapter 9, "No More Nightmares," for my thoughts about bedside tables.)

All the pieces that might be useful in a bedroom, such as storage units, headboards, dressers, and shelving components, need to be carefully measured so that you can actually fit your belongings into them.

ORGANIZED MEANS SAFE

Be sure you create not only an organized home, but a safe one, especially if you have children around. Make provisions to take care of the following items:

- Fire extinguishers
- Smoke alarms
- Safety strips for bathtubs and showers
- Grip bars for tubs and showers
- Childproof latches for cupboards and drawers
- Locks on medicine chests
- Plugs for electric outlets
- Pads to cushion table corners
- Bookcases—and other pieces of furniture children might climb on—bolted to the walls
- Child gates at doors and stairs
- Fence or secure cover for swimming pool

EQUIPPING THE KITCHEN

After reading the kitchen chapter (Chapter 10, "Calmly Cut Down Kitchen Clutter"), you'll be inspired to use several organizing tools to keep things pared down in that usually busy room. On your list of big-ticket items, consider the following additions to make your kitchen lived-in, loved, and livable.

YOU'LL THANK YOURSELF LATER

Try to use one or two big matching pieces of bedroom furniture instead of a baker's dozen of tables, bookcases, and assorted extras on which to perch your stuff. Things will look so much more organized and serene.

IF YOU'RE SO
INCLINED

Consider replacing bulky, old, space-stealing appliances with new, smaller ones. Newly designed microwaves, coffeemakers, and blenders have thinner profiles and smaller "footprints" and just look sleeker.

A rolling cart can be a great helper, acting almost as a second pair of hands to hold things while you do your kitchen chores. Carts can be made of wood or steel wire, and may have shelves or a cupboard arrangement below a butcher block top or other surface material. Scoot your cart in from a hallway, pantry, or corridor and use it as another work surface or storage spot. They're great!

If you've got the room, a small file cabinet in the kitchen ensnares kitchen and food-related paperwork: recipes, obviously, but also meal plans, shopping lists, entertainment ideas, health and nutrition information, and warranties and instruction booklets for kitchen gear.

Getting Time on Your Side

	The Old Way	The Lazy Way
Buying the right computer for your needs	Oops! (Darn!)	A few hours
Finding the tools you need	Weeks	A few days
Labeling your stuff	Hours	30 minutes
Finding stuff in your closets	Never!	A few minutes
Making sure your home is child-safe	A losing battle	A few hours
Finding your grandmother's recipe for stuffing	Could take years	2 seconds!

Part 2

Organize Without Agony

Are you too lazy to read Organize Without Agony?

1 You buy more belated birthday cards than regular ones.
☐ yes ☐ no

2 You could have sent a child to college with the fees you've paid for late credit card payments. ☐ yes ☐ no

3 Your technique for getting rid of paper is to lose it.
☐ yes ☐ no

Tricks of the Trade

If this is your first serious attempt to get organized, begin by making an appointments with yourself to start making good on your commitment. You'll need to block two- to three-hour periods, which is enough time to see some real progress but not—I hope—enough to exhaust you.

You might pick a room or an area to begin with. Pick something that's really been affecting your productivity or peace of mind. Go to that chapter in this book and read it through. After getting an idea of what you'll be doing, get the supplies and equipment you don't have. Get more supplies than you think you'll need—it's better to have too many of something (like file folders) than to run out mid-project. You can always use or return the unused items later.

As always, the most important preparation you can make is to get rid of the stuff you know needs to be tossed. It may take you several sessions to just do the purging, but like painting, you've got to do the groundwork. Weeding out is the single most important organizing task you can do. If you've done that, you can use your work session to make order, not make decisions!

Have a small stash of mailing supplies on hand: large envelopes, shipping labels, perhaps even some boxes. That way, if you need to mail papers to their rightful owner, ship used clothes to your nephews, or distribute presents you bought and never gave away, you can make fast work of getting those projects handled.

Then follow the steps outlined in the chapter you're working on, using those tips you can use immediately, or those that are appropriate for your particular situation, and do them. You will see, I promise, enormous changes in your physical space and feel incredibly lightened. Remember: (1) This exercise will pay enormous dividends down the road; (2) stick with it; and (3) organizing projects usually look worse before they get better.

SYSTEMS THAT WORK

Not specific to a particular area of the office or home, but worthy of your attention, is making routine chores as systematized as you can. Think of things you do regularly that can be done at least partly in advance. You might save just a few minutes, but those minutes add up. The following sections outline some routines and how they can be speeded up. For example, anything you write down regularly can be handled in several ways. Think carefully about what you need to write down all the time and see if there is a way to shorten or automate the process.

Reliable Rubber Stamps to the Rescue

Rubber stamps are great. Have them made up for any information you need to regularly distribute; a small

QUICK ⬤ PAINLESS

If you frequently need to take papers to the copy center or office for photocopying, assign a bright-colored folder to collect the next batch. Keep the folder by the door or in a bag or briefcase that goes out with you.

investment saves you oodles of time. Get the self-inking kind so you don't need to fool with stamp pads anymore. Stamps have a multitude of uses:

- Use them for your return address, of course.

- Instead of printing new stationery or new business cards, could you make do with a rubber stamp with your new fax number or e-mail address?

- Use a stamp with each child's name for their paper lunch bags, folders, or whatever.

Then use your stamps to stamp a supply of lunch bags (the kids will have fun doing this themselves) or forms all at once. The things you need will be there for you, ready to go, when you need them.

Envelopes to Go

Another advance chore: Prepare a supply of envelopes ahead of time to anyone or any company you send things to regularly. You can use the computer for this task, or use your return address stamp. Think how much faster it would go if you had envelopes prepared for:

- Aunt Tilly, to whom you often send clippings and articles

- Your health insurance claims office

- Anyone to whom you pay a bill regularly who does not supply an envelope

Come bill-paying time, you can grab an envelope and speed through the process without stopping to prepare an envelope. And instead of having articles for Aunt Tilly

YOU'LL THANK YOURSELF LATER

Start stamping your way through life and save yourself countless hours of time, and never suffer hand cramp again!

spread all over your desk, you can put them directly into a pre-addressed envelope. You'll be much more likely to send things often if you've got envelopes waiting at the ready.

Label Mania

Order return address labels, and put your telephone number on them. I think rubber stamps are faster than address labels for envelopes, but sticky labels are handy for identifying books, videos, small tools, dishes going to the potluck dinner, and other belongings. I like the clear ones.

Order shipping labels with your return name and address on them. They are about three inches high by four inches wide and should be self-sticking; you can order them on rolls or in sheets. You'll find them invaluable every time you need to return a catalog order or have a box or large envelope to mail. Slap one on, write in the recipient's name and address, and you're done.

More Automation for Numbers and Forms

If you regularly fill out insurance claim forms, make a master, filling in all the information that stays the same each time. Make copies of it, and you'll never have to fill out the routine information again.

Typing out telephone lists can be handy by saving you the time it takes to look up numbers. (And if you use the computer for this chore, you can update these lists regularly and quickly.) For example:

- Type your frequently used telephone numbers and post them by the telephone. (This is handy for children, too, allowing them to do their own telephoning without your help.) Imagine never having to look up the telephone numbers of the video store, the pizza parlor, or the library again.

- Do the same for fax numbers and keep your list close to the fax machine.

- I've made a list of phone numbers that I dial from my cell phone in the car, using large bold type. I use bright paper, so I can find it quickly, and put it into a plastic sheet protector. (You know, of course, that you don't want to be looking up numbers and drivin' and dialin' at the same time.)

- Spend the time necessary to program your telephone speed dial buttons. You will save many minutes every day by not having to dial frequently called clients, friends, or suppliers. If you have a fax, program those numbers, too.

THE ALL-IMPORTANT ORGANIZER

Your date book/calendar is one of the most useful tools you can have, if you use it regularly and properly. It is essential that you have just one (with one exception that I'll mention later). Trying to keep two or more calendars constantly updated is time-consuming and frustrating. If you write down everything you need to know or remember in this one place, you'll find your life will get much easier.

A COMPLETE WASTE OF TIME

The 3 Worst Things You Can Do When it Comes to Your Important Numbers Are:

1. Keep them on tiny scraps of paper

2. Don't post them in an accessible place

3. Put off organizing them until "tomorrow"

The purpose of getting your date book organized and using it regularly is to save you from having to remember things. You want your head to be clear to be creative, to relax, or to concentrate on the chore at hand—not to be vaguely wondering if you missed an appointment with the vet this morning or if that report was due this week or next.

Choosing a date book is important; it has to work for you and your particular needs. You can use any type of date book you like, taking into consideration the amount of space you need to write things down. Some people need a whole page per day; others can manage a whole month on two small pages. Hole-punched pages are a good idea so you can add and subtract pages—such as address pages or blank pages for taking notes—as you need them in a binder.

Get a date book as small as possible so that you can cart it around with you. Sounds annoying, maybe, but if you have it with you, you can make appointments on the spot, instead of running home or to the office, checking your calendar, and then having to make another phone call to set up an appointment. Carrying it with you will save you a lot of steps. If you don't regularly carry a briefcase, look for a date book with a cover that has a shoulder strap.

You can find date books ranging from simple, inexpensive ones with plastic covers all the way to refill systems contained in fine-quality leather portfolios with shoulder straps. Day-Timer™, FranklinCovey™ Planners, Filofax™, and DayRunner™ offer systems with paper

refills in virtually any format you'd need. You can add address book pages, expense report pages, mileage tracking, or voice mail records to fully customize your date book. There are sleeves for computer floppy disks and holders for tiny calculators.

In addition, you can stick a plastic pouch in your binder where you can stash a credit card, some cash, or a checkbook, and your date book will be able to go with you anywhere, in one hand, saving you from the bulging pocket syndrome or carrying a purse.

If you're computerized, there are several good calendering software programs available. Check them out and pick one that meets your specific needs.

Another way to get yourself organized, manage your time, and keep track of people and numbers is to use an electronic organizer (or PIM—Personal Information Manager). The current market favorites are 3Com's PalmPilot and Palm III. (The Palm III has the most features and largest capacity; for simplicity's sake, I'm calling both versions "PalmPilots.")

Big Little Helpers

These battery-operated devices weigh less than 6 oz., so they certainly make the grade as far as portability is concerned. But it's what you can do with them that is the big news: they can keep 5 years of appointments, 6000 addresses, 1500 "to do" entries (heaven forbid!) and written records and email messages. You can use them by themselves or easily transfer data to them from your desktop computer.

IF YOU'RE SO
INCLINED

Before you go out and buy an organizer that may or may not work for your personal needs, let your fingers do the walking. Talk to a few distributors and get their input. That way, when you do set out to actually acquire one of these handy helpers, you won't have wasted a day in the process!

QUICK **🔲** PAINLESS

The most remarkable feature, however, of the PalmPilot is the fact that you can actually write, with a little stylus, on the screen surface. What you write is magically transformed into print on the screen.

So, you carry this little guy around with you in a pouch, pull it out to add an address of someone you just met, search your addresses to see what other contacts you have in that company, tap on the screen to look at today's schedule, and then bring up the week so you can visually scan the whole week's appointments. Then make notes from your meeting and jot down your expense items and amounts.

If you need to, you can quickly exchange information to and from your desktop computer and your PalmPilot. Your database on your computer will get the new address you just added and expense information. And your PalmPilot can pick up and store your email messages.

Here are several ways to use your date book, beyond the scheduling of daily appointments, to maximize its effectiveness:

- At the beginning of every year, jot down next year's birthdays that you want to remember in next year's date book (or let your computer software do it for you). Use a colored pen so they stand out. It'll take about 10 minutes, and there will be one less thing to remember all year!

- Make appointments to perform home and auto maintenance chores: clean the refrigerator coils, replace furnace filters, clean stove and microwave vents, check the water filter, and so on. Make a note to yourself about when your next car service is due or when you should schedule your next teeth-cleaning.

- As soon as the kids come home with papers noting school days off, school concert dates, early dismissals, and holidays, write them in your date book immediately.

- Make appointments with yourself to read, to meditate, to exercise, to plan, and to organize. These are what Stephen R. Covey, author of *The 7 Habits of Highly Effective People*, would call "Quadrant II activities" (important, but not urgent) on his Time Management Matrix. It seems that the only way to fit these activities into your life is to schedule them. If you don't give them priority, there will always be other activities to preclude doing them. Writing them down in your date book gives them more "weight" and you can schedule around them more easily.

- Alongside your appointments, keep a list of what you'd like to accomplish each day. If you write a reminder to "Call Bob," be sure and write down his telephone number. It makes it easier to squeeze in the phone call between appointments or during a short break.

The Exception to the Rule

The one exception to using just one calendar is that you might want a large monthly calendar for noting family

You've done it! You've got a date book. You know where you're supposed to be all week. You know whom you have to call in the next month. Now make an appointment with yourself to steal away to browse a bookstore in the middle of the day or to get a massage midweek. Enjoy!

The Lazy Way

Everyday, check your personal date book against the family calendar on the refrigerator. Add family events to your personal one and update the family calendar with your personal activities that will impact others. The few extra minutes you spend doing this, in an ideal world, will keep everyone in the know!

events in a central place in your home (usually the kitchen). This way, everyone can keep track of what affects some or all of the family. The same technique applies to the office: A two- or three-month display calendar can serve as a "big picture" reminder of vacations and trips, as well as start and completion dates for long projects.

Getting Time on Your Side

	The Old Way	**The Lazy Way**
Making sure everyone knows about the family reunion	Almost impossible	2 seconds
Finding the fax number you need	2 hours	2 seconds
Finding your weekly shipment of recipes for your niece	1 hour	1 minute
Getting the stuff together to pay your bills	30 minutes	5 minutes
Sorting out whose lunch is whose in the morning	10 minutes	No time at all!
Finding time to relax	Who's got time?	Tomorrow afternoon—you planned for it!

In Short Order

We all want to save time, and one way to do that is either eliminate some of the things we do or shorten the time we spend doing things that must be done. This chapter offers suggestions for both approaches. Of course, not every suggestion will work for you or make sense, so be selective, and take and use what works for you.

ON THE ROAD

If you travel often, be it to the Far East or Flushing, set up some systems in place to make getting out the door as easy as possible:

- Pack your shaving kit or cosmetic case with everything you need for a getaway. Keep it in your bathroom or bureau so you can grab it on a moment's notice.

- Keep a small cosmetic case in your car or office so you can always make emergency touch-ups.

- Men might keep a small case—packed with extra razor, shaving cream, toothbrush, and toothpaste—at the office or in the car.

- Zip-locking bags are great for packing. The teeny "snack size" (about 6½ inches by 3¼ inches) are terrific for pills or jewelry. Pack folded sweaters in their own bags and all your underwear in another.

- Pack an extra couple of large plastic bags to hold dirty laundry and wet towels or bathing suits.

- I always pack for an airplane trip with a change of underwear, cosmetics, and prescriptions in my carry-on luggage, just in case I end up stranded and have to spend an unplanned-for night in a hotel. If there's room, I sometimes roll up a pair of sweatpants or extra T-shirt and stuff that in as well.

ERRANDS AND CHORES

Think ahead. Consolidate errands and chores whenever possible. Group several things to do at one end of town, or save up the things you want to do at the library, for example, and do them all at once.

Group activities so that you're close at hand to other family members; for example, do some cleanup in the garage if your spouse is mowing the lawn, or do some reading in your child's room while he or she does homework.

In the Car

- Keep a pad of sticky notes in the car; jot things down as they occur to you and stick the note to something such as your briefcase or purse. That way, it makes it into the house or office with you.

- If you often make deliveries and have to keep directions to different addresses, put them together in a small loose-leaf binder in your car.

- Keep a list of frequently called telephone numbers on a sheet of paper in your car.

- I always have books on tape in my car for any drive longer than 20 minutes or for when I get stuck in traffic. From mysteries to self-help and business, they make driving time enjoyable and productive.

A PAPER WARDROBE

We all need to constantly give our names, addresses, and telephone numbers—not to mention fax numbers, pager numbers, and e-mail addresses—to others as we go about our lives. You will save time and cut down on the chance of mistakes communicating this information to others by having a selection of paper products customized just for you. You will certainly *look* more organized and can also use these products to project a good image. Here's a list of some helpful components of a paper wardrobe:

- I advise clients—absolutely everyone—to get business cards. Even if you're not in business and have no more than a telephone number, you need business cards. They save you and others confusion, and preclude the need for scribbling on scraps of paper or finding a number jotted down with no name attached to it. Whether you're networking in a business situation or dropping clothes off at the

IF YOU'RE SO INCLINED

Is your car your office more often than not? Then outfit it for business with some Post-It notes and a binder of frequently needed information and it will be much easier to keep the show on the road!

cleaners, pulling out your card communicates the information others need to know quickly and accurately. You can get them printed up inexpensively at your local printer or office-supply stores, and you can also make your own at home with a printer and word processing program.

- Another item you should order is envelopes with your name and address on them. They're handy for bill-paying, for forwarding material to someone, or for jotting down notes on paper that has no matching envelope. I'd suggest using a #10 envelope—the business size—to accommodate 8½ by 11 inch sheets of paper. Again, office-supply stores and local printers can help you out.

- Then there's stationery with all your information on it. Obviously, if you're in business, you already have letterhead. But again, if you're living, you're in business of some kind, and a note to the mortgage company or your child's teacher requires the same information. Get it in print.

- Nice stationery can be a motivator to correspond by—gasp!—handwriting. You know, pen to paper. These days, that's almost unheard of, and it's a lovely gesture to the recipient. Besides, if you like this sort of thing, designing your own stationery can be a creative project, and the result will be a reflection of your style and personality. You can order stationery anywhere from the local printer (quick and inexpensive) to Tiffany's best (engraved and pricey).

YOU'LL THANK YOURSELF LATER

Two words: Business Cards. No matter what you do, a business card is the easiest way to make a lasting impression, and keep you in touch!

- I have pads made up, with all the pertinent numbers on them, for quick notes. Ask your local copy center or Kinko's to print four on a page, cut into fourths, and pad each stack. They'll save you a lot of time.

- Correspondence cards are handy to have on hand. If they're printed, you can grab one, jot down your note or thank you message, and send it off—quickly and to the point.

- I ordered personalized postcards from American Stationers (see Appendix A, "How to Get Someone Else to Do It"). The cards have my name and address on them in a pretty color. I use them so often that I don't know how I survived without them! They require less postage, too.

- If you don't already have a box of generic birthday cards or attractive all-purpose cards, get some to have on hand.

TIME MANAGEMENT

To quickly respond to a fax or letter, just jot your response down on the original, take a copy if necessary, and either fax or send back the original. You've saved time and paper.

Try to plan your most demanding work when you're most productive, paying attention to your personal daily rhythm. That means mornings for most people should be saved for the hard or creative stuff and late afternoons for routine chores (filing or entering information into your database, for example).

Congratulations! You've had personalized stationery made up with all your numbers on them so that people don't have to hunt for your phone number when they need you! Now, give yourself a break, turn the ringer off, and steal a quick catnap!

The Lazy Way

Be conscious of what you need to do. Make the distinction between what's urgent and what's important. Read Stephen R. Covey's book, *The 7 Habits of Highly Effective People*, to help you prioritize the important things in your life (which are not necessarily the urgent ones) and use your time wisely to accomplish them.

Always schedule more time than you think you'll need as you make appointments, set deadlines, or block out time lines for completing projects. Even something as simple (and common) as a dentist running late can ruin your whole day and increase your stress level unnecessarily. Had you allowed yourself two hours instead of one, and the appointment took one and a half hours, you could have relaxed with a cup of coffee and the newspaper or made a few extra phone calls with your "extra" half hour.

All of us have projects we'd like to work on and finish at some point. Unfortunately, because these projects don't have deadlines, they sometimes never get finished. Set deadlines for yourself and see if things don't move forward. You can either set a date for the completion of your project or break up the project into steps and set deadlines for each step. Be sure to write these dates into your calendar.

Use the time you spend chatting on the telephone with a friend (or a boring relative) to accomplish something else. I always use my portable phone if I know I'm going to be on the phone more than, say, 10 minutes, and don't have to particularly concentrate on the

A COMPLETE WASTE OF TIME

The 3 Worst Things You Can Do When it Comes to Planning Your Day Are:

1. Ignore your personal daily rhythm: If you're not on the ball in the morning then save the number crunching for the afternoon!

2. Categorize everything as Priority One—who needs the ulcer?

3. Try and cram everything into ten minute slots—Nothing gets done that fast!

conversation. I attack the junk drawer, empty the refrigerator of anything green that shouldn't be, wipe the stove top, or do some filing.

Not a shortcut, maybe, but a good idea anyway: Get up an hour earlier one morning a week. Use that time to get some reading done, work on your novel, take a brisk walk, or write a short letter or two.

At the end of every day, or as you're leaving your work area, jot down a to-do list for the following day. You'll already have non-negotiable appointments (such as a session with your accountant) in your date book, so your list will be what has to get done and the extras that you hope to accomplish.

FOOD

If you have the space—and you should once you've read this book and begun a new era of purging—buy food staples and household supplies in bulk. Canned goods, paper products, and toiletries can all be on hand when you need them. You should also pay less for some items if they're priced by the case.

Cook and bake double portions; freeze half for another meal.

Make two dishes from the same main ingredient. Two pounds of hamburger could be divided to make hamburgers one night and spaghetti sauce the next.

Prepare a couple of entrees (a lasagna and a stew, for example) on the weekend. Divide into meal-sized portions and freeze or refrigerate. As you drag yourself

IF YOU'RE SO
INCLINED

Here's a nifty idea that can save you many trips to run errands. Make up a small notebook—or use a couple of pages in your date book—to keep track of model numbers and refill numbers for your equipment and appliances, such as the fax machine (so you know what size paper to buy), your vacuum cleaner (so you purchase the right dust bag), and your computer printer and copier (so you have their toner and ink cartridge numbers with you while you're at the office-supply store).

home after a tiring day, you can take comfort in the fact that the hardest part of dinner is already done.

Handling Lunch

Save money and take your lunch to work if practical. Simplify by creating a lunch menu for yourself (as you did for the kids' lunches), so you don't have to be inventive at 6:00 a.m. List a combination of foods for every day of the week, or five different choices to make depending upon what you've got in the house. Hopefully you often have leftovers that can be packed, too.

Down the Hatch

In a hurry? Try drinking your meals. (No, I don't mean three martinis!) At the office, between meetings, in airplanes or airports and on the road: you can keep yourself fueled and alert by using prepared drink mixes. And you'll be less tempted to use the vending machines filled with candy and soft drinks!

There are healthy and palatable powders on the market which, when mixed with juice or water, will keep you going until the next solid meal. Ask friends, relatives or workout mavens what they recommend. A session with a nutritionist would also be helpful in choosing products to complement your regular diet.

Quick Whisk

A handy gadget my friend Mary Kay swears by is a small, portable, battery-operated whisk that she takes with her everywhere. She explains that spoons don't do a very

IF YOU'RE SO INCLINED

If a portable liquid diet sounds like the perfect solution for those hectic days, make sure you don't short yourself on important nutrients. Schedule a brief session with a local nutritionist and describe your needs to them. That way you can still have a lazy solution that will also feed you properly!

good job of mixing powders, and her little device is a powerhouse! It comes from Matol Botanical International, and is called a shaker mixer. It costs all of $5.00!

PICTURES 'N' PHOTOS

The subject of photographs and how to manage them is worthy of a book unto itself, but here are some ideas to start using now:

- As you get new photos developed, immediately label the envelope with the occasion, events, and dates relevant to that batch of pictures.

- Toss the rejects.

- I've yet to meet anyone who does this, but I've heard of people who take their photo album pages with them on trips. They have their pictures developed while at their vacation spot or during their travels and assemble album pages before they even get home! It makes sense: Vacations may be the only time to do projects like this. Worth a try!

A great resource that might inspire you to deal with your many shoeboxes filled with snapshots is to take a class. There are companies whose only mission is to see that you have every photograph you've ever taken (and want to keep) properly taken care of.

Creative Memories is one of those companies. Not long ago, I spent a wonderful evening with one of their representatives who gathered a group of us together

QUICK ⬤ PAINLESS

If you can no longer avoid entertaining (and assuming cooking is low on your list of priorities), my advice is to cheat. Order the entree from a local restaurant. You'll just have to prepare a salad and bake a potato or make rice. If you can convince one of your guests that you can't live without her dessert, you've got a dinner party handled!

All those photos that have been sitting in boxes for years are important, so don't let them languish unattended! Sure, it will take some time at first, but you'll end up with a beautiful record of all those important moments in your life. It's worth it!

and reminded us of how important our photographs are—or will be—for generations to come. She also taught us the value of journalizing—writing down the who, the what, and the where of our pictures—because those future generations aren't going to have a clue who we are, let alone who our best friends are in our pictures!

You can buy products from Creative Memories, as well as tools to make your job easier and more creative. All their paper products are acid-free and meant to protect your photographs for a long time. The creative part comes with the stickers, patterned background papers, cutters and scissors with decorative blades and stick-on letters.

Our class ended up around a table, cutting and pasting the photos we had brought with us, recalling our days as artists in kindergarten! If you need inspiration and the tools and materials to make it happen, try a class to get you started.

OTHER CLEVER WAYS TO GET THINGS DONE

Buy stamps by mail from the post office and skip the lines.

Save space, save resources, and save money: Use the library. If, after reading a book, you decide you must own it, go out and purchase it. All those one-time-only books will not have cost you anything, nor will they sit around taking up your space.

Stop shopping, even if something's on sale, two-for-the-price-of-one, affordable, the last one, new, or antique. If you don't need it, you shouldn't bring it home. Always remember the cost of owning things, and the more you own, the more you have to organize and take care of.

Use the services your bank offers to your best advantage. Set up direct deposits for anything you can, including payroll checks, dividends, Social Security, and so on. You'll need to call the issuer of these checks, sign a form, and give them a voided blank check to set things up, but you have to do that only once. And it saves the time you now spend writing out deposit slips, endorsing your checks, getting to the bank, and getting to the front of the line.

To pay bills, get on an automatic deduction schedule for anything you can. You can pay your mortgage, insurance, utilities, telephone, and more this way, saving you a big chunk of time and postage at bill-paying time.

Consider online banking, then you can do your banking at any time that is convenient for you. Online banking also allows you to pay your bills electronically, and you can schedule them for automatic payment at the same time each month. Look ma, no more envelopes to mail!

MORE MINUTE-SAVERS

Instead of trying to fit everything you need to do between the hours of 9 to 5, make breakfast or evening appointments, especially if you're a morning person or a night owl. You can meet your event co-chairs for

Congratulations! You've turned your banking nightmare into an electronic dream! Treat yourself to an afternoon with your favorite book!

Plan. Make an appointment with yourself (and write it in your calendar) for an hour or so once a week, or every couple of weeks, to just think and plan the next few weeks or months. Planning is one of the best uses of your time, and you'll accomplish much more by mapping out what you want to do and when. I've read that one hour of planning can save you three hours of work.

breakfast and go over what's to be done, and your insurance broker or computer consultant might be happy to accommodate you after dinner some evening.

Do errands at odd times. Grocery shop, fill up the car with gas, and return library books at midnight if you want and if you're still on your feet. You surely won't spend any time waiting in line at those places at that hour!

MAINTENANCE PROJECTS

Every single suggestion or procedure mentioned in this book is like all good habits: It must be done regularly. A house will eventually collapse into the ground if you don't care for it and keep it up. It's the same with your organizational systems. If you don't keep on top of these following tasks, it will take you a lot of time to dig out:

- File your papers regularly. Remember the rule: If you're in doubt, toss it, especially if you know someone else has it.

- Go through your clothes with purging on your mind once every season. (Make an appointment in your calendar.) If you're about to put away an outfit you haven't worn all season, it should probably go in the give-away pile.

- Have a garage sale, or organize a neighborhood sale, once a year. Get everyone in the family to go through their belongings and contribute items. Just don't come home with a new collection of junk!

Go through kids' toys and clothing at least twice a year. They tend to accumulate so much stuff so quickly, and they need regular help to keep the decks clear.

THE ART OF GIFT GIVING

Giving gifts can be a real hassle to some folks. Some people never have the time to shop for gifts in an organized fashion, so they end up with expensive mistakes purchased at the last minute. Others buy gifts all the time, but they seem to collect all over the house and never seem to get "given." The following sections offer a few tips for gift shopping and giving that may make your life easier.

Stay Out of Stores

Retailers will hate me for saying this, but when you're buying gifts for several people at a time, cruising the mall is the least efficient method of accomplishing this. There are other options, though; if you want gifts from a specific store, call the store and ask them to pluck, wrap, and then send your gifts for you. I do this for things I don't have to pick out, like books. Call your bookstore and ask for titles by name and arrange the whole project on the phone. And here are some more alternatives for you:

- Catalogs. Take advantage of their wrapping and shipping services.

QUICK ⬤ PAINLESS

If you've created a new filing system, it should now be organized in logical order so it's easy to find things. But if you're of the school that believes, "If I can't see it on the top of my desk, I'll forget it," make a map of your file system. On a piece of paper or index card, simply list the categories you've set up and then list the folders underneath those headings. Make a card like this for each file drawer and tape it to the outside of the corresponding file drawer. That way, you can look at your map to either retrieve something or to put a file away in the proper place.

- Ask retailers or catalogs to send gift certificates. The recipient can then choose his or her own gift.

- Use the Internet.

- If you already have a collection of gifts, put them all together in a plastic box or bin and pull them out as you need them.

Having said all that, my advice is *not* to give presents in the traditional sense. How many people do you know who actually *need* more things? We live in such an affluent, consumer-oriented society that we actually have to write books about getting rid of things. Don't add to the problem. There are lots of wonderful, useful, and creative gifts you can give that won't add to the world's trash pile—or strain your budget!

- Give services: a massage or a manicure to your stressed-out friends, a couple of hours of a computer consultant's time to a budding entrepreneur, an image consultant's time to a sister reentering the work force.

- Give your own services: an evening's baby-sitting for new (or veteran) parents, a day's worth of painting to the new apartment dweller, haircuts for your friend's kids.

- Give entertainment: tickets to the movies, a play, concerts, or dance performances.

- Give green things: a tree to a new home-owner, a selection of annuals from the nursery and your labor

A COMPLETE WASTE OF TIME

The 3 Worst Things You Can Do When it Comes to Gift Giving Are:

1. Save your gift shopping for the very last minute

2. Ignore the resources on the Internet

3. Forget to get one altogether

planting them to a single mom, a beautiful pot in which you've planted a gorgeous indoor plant as a birthday present to your boss.

- Give food: your most beloved chocolate chip cookies or loaf of bread presented in a pretty basket, a gift basket with goodies from the gourmet shop, a great bottle of wine.

WRAPPING IT ALL UP

Buy wrapping paper in bulk—in just one or two colors or patterns—for all your gift-giving. Buy just a few types of ribbon that go with each of the papers. If you pick attractive papers that are solid or non-themed, you will always have appropriate wrapping on hand for boys, grandmothers, new babies, or husbands. Just think how simple!

I've chosen wide, white shelf paper for one of my gift wraps. Then I use a red ribbon for Christmas or Valentine's Day, yellow for baby shower gifts, and silver or gold for girlfriends and wedding presents.

Consider newspaper as a gift wrap; tie with red raffia for a colorful touch!

Another great-looking (and inexpensive) gift paper is butcher paper (you know—plain brown wrapping paper). You can buy huge rolls of it, and it has lots of uses. Use a shiny black ribbon to go with it—very sophisticated.

QUICK ☻ PAINLESS

If you've got an oversized gift to wrap, use a paper tablecloth—so much easier than piecing together smaller lengths of paper. You'll find paper tablecloths next to paper plates in colors and patterns appropriate for the season or occasion.

PACK YOUR BAGS!

Use plastic bags to organize smaller items: the stray birthday candles, the collection of seashells, an assortment of tacks and pushpins. Ziplock "Snack Bags" are 6½ inches wide by 3¼ inches, and are just perfect for packing jewelry, pills, and so forth.

Would it make sense for you to keep your gym bag in the laundry area? That way, your soggy sweats can go directly from bag to washer and dryer and back into the bag.

MOVING

If there were ever a time you wanted to be organized, it's before, during and after a move. But it needn't be one of life's most terrible events if you've got a system. Here it is, *The Lazy Way:*

Start Now

Everything I've ever told you about throwing things away will come back to haunt you during a move. If you've ignored me so far, this is your big chance to go through your belongings and get rid of anything you're in doubt about keeping. There is no point in spending time packing things you don't want, having to move them (requiring both space and money) and then having to unpack them at the other end. You know the routine by now: things should go in the trash, to the thrift shop, consignment store, be given away to friends or relatives, or recycled. Start early, sorting and tossing—well before you start packing.

Make a Plan, Stan

First of all, you want to make a plan. On paper. Determine your deadline—the day the moving trucks roll up to your garage door—and work backward from that date.

How you plan your move is going to depend upon how much time you have 'til moving day and how much help you are hiring. You may have the movers pack everything you own, which will certainly mean a different time line than if you are doing everything yourself.

Break It Up

Whatever tasks you have to do, break them down into smaller jobs. Don't write "Pack the household" on your to do list—you'll collapse from stress if you read that every day. Instead, make a list of small jobs: "pack books," "pack garage," "pack pots and pans," etc. Write these jobs in your planner and give them deadlines. Much easier and more manageable.

Make your arrangements earlier than you think necessary; there's nothing more frustrating than a snappy clerk telling you that everything is booked and you can't get an appointment until a week after you need one. Here are some of the calls or arrangements you may need to make before the move:

- Hire your mover.
- Call your utility companies well in advance to arrange for cut-off dates. If you have cable TV equipment, return it or have it picked up to avoid rental charges.

YOU'LL THANK YOURSELF LATER

The absolutely first secret to a smooth move is throwing out every last thing you possibly can. This is the time to be tough, because you're going to hate packing and then unpacking that old pair of skis which you haven't used for years, and which you won't know where to store in your new digs.

- Arrange for the telephone to be disconnected—a couple of days *after* you move.

- Be sure and leave enough time to clean, or arrange for cleaning to be done after you leave.

- Deal with the post office: give them a change of address form so that your mail gets forwarded with no interruption starting the day you specify.

- Send change of address cards as early as practical to your friends, relatives and anyone you do business with. (Be sure and note your new telephone and fax numbers on your cards to friends.) Your subscriptions need a particularly long lead-time.

- Order new stationery, bill-paying envelopes and return address stamp or labels with your new address on them.

- Let your insurance company know of your moving plans and how they might impact your vehicles and belongings.

Packing With Purpose

Okay, it's never been fun, but it's not brain surgery. If you're doing the packing, you'll make it easier on yourself with the right supplies at hand. These may include:

- Boxes, taped securely at the bottoms (inquire at your local moving company if they have used boxes available for sale).

Congratulations! You've equipped yourself with everything you need to get cracking on the packing! Now, before you jump into the fray, treat yourself to a nice cup of tea!

The Lazy Way

- Special containers (also from the moving company) in which to pack clothes—they are tall boxes with a hanging rod at the top on which to place hangers.

- Framed pictures and paintings need special boxes, too, to protect them.

- Several rolls of tape (each in a different color).

- Wide tape dispenser.

- Big, broad-nibbed marker pens.

- Newspaper or packing paper (from the moving company).

Use the rolls of different colored tape (found at your local hardware store) to identify boxes that go in different rooms. This will be an easy visual clue to whomever is moving boxes in.

Survival of the Fittest

If you experience the worst-case scenario, you'll arrive in the middle of the night to a cold house, hungry and tired. Here's what to pack to ensure your survival the first 24 hours:

- Pack one box for immediate kitchen use on arrival: tea bags or individual filter packs for coffee, soup mixes, instant cocoa, crackers, some fruit, energy bars, juice packs, and snacks for children. Add a roll of paper towels, paper plates and cups, and plastic utensils. Label clearly and either put it in the truck last, or take it with you.

YOU'LL THANK YOURSELF LATER

Color code your stuff! Whether you do it with colored tape or colored markers, breaking your household down into colors will make moving much easier! No more hunting through boxes for a specific item! Besides, it will also make it easier for your movers to know which box goes where!

In all the confusion of moving, don't forget to have the movers' payment with you at your destination. Imagine how you'd feel seeing them drive off again with all your belongings until the bank opens on Monday!

▨ Pack another box for immediate bedding needs. Designate sleeping bags for kids, one set of sheets and blankets per adult, and one towel per person.

▨ Add, well-packed in plastic bags, a box with everyone's toothbrushes, toothpaste, shampoo, and soap. And don't forget toilet paper!

▨ Have a small box of tools with you; include a hammer, screwdrivers, a carton cutter, and duct tape. (I'd advise tacks or pushpins, too—you never know when you'll need to use a sheet as a curtain!)

▨ A phone! Don't pack all your telephones!

▨ Don't forget a few basic cleaning supplies: rags, gloves, cleansers, a broom, mop, and dustpan.

▨ Pack your "Important Papers," "Family Life," and "End of Life" binders and take them with you. You will minimize the risk of losing them, and you most likely will need some of their information in your new location.

Plan ahead for the other end of the line: here's a checklist of things to do before you land. Have these things in order and you'll be safe and sane when you arrive at your new home:

▨ Make hotel arrangements if you need them.

▨ Arrange with utility companies to turn on your utilities on the appropriate date.

▨ Be sure your telephone service is ordered well in advance. Make sure you have the right number of lines and that the phone jacks are in the right places in your new house.

- Make arrangements so your long distance carrier service is uninterrupted.
- Book a date with your cable guy.
- Ask your computer guru what needs to be done to safely transport your equipment and what needs to be installed at the other end to accommodate it all.
- Make a floor plan of your new house and have a good idea of what's going to go where. At least figure out in advance where the big items are going to be placed, saving you and the movers a lot of last-minute creative interior design upon arrival.
- Find out in advance how to register your children in school so you'll be prepared on their first school day.
- Open up at least one bank account in your new town. Order checks with your new address on them.
- Change your address with your motor vehicle department.
- Let Social Security know where you're going. The number is 800/772-1213.
- Register to vote!

F.Y.I. re: the U.S.P.S.

That means, here's what you need to know about what the post office will handle, for how long, and (most) at no charge:

IF YOU'RE SO
INCLINED

If you are taking rugs, upholstered furniture or drapes with you to your new house, have them picked up for cleaning right before the move. Have them delivered back to your new house!

Congratulations! You did it! You planned, made a moving schedule, and stuck to it! Arrange for a cleaning service to come and do a once-over in your new house before the movers arrive. Even if the former tenants said they cleaned, there's almost always more to do. So see to it that you come home to a nice, clean place.

The Lazy Way

1. First-class, priority and express mail will be forwarded for 12 months.

2. Newspapers and magazines will be forwarded for 60 days.

3. Packages over 1 pound will be forward locally for 12 months. If your packages need to be forwarded out of the area, you pay forwarding charges.

4. You have to ask your post office specifically to have books, catalogs, and advertising mail forwarded.

5. If you receive mail with a yellow label attached to it, be sure and let the sender know your new address; they don't have it.

Delegate or, "I'm Going to Have a Nervous Breakdown"

You may find it worth the expense to hire a moving coordinator to handle all the details listed in these pages. A coordinator will oversee the packing, moving and unpacking of your belongings and make the myriad arrangements that need to be handled. This should assure you of a much smoother move, a quicker settling in to your new house, and less time missed at work and school.

Look in the yellow pages for moving coordinators and professional organizers, and ask moving companies for suggestions.

HOUSE FOR SALE

If you're moving, you very likely may have a house to sell. You can increase your chances of a quick sell—and a higher price—by giving your place a quick facelift. Real estate specialists always say you're almost assured of getting your investment back by making these improvements.

Creating Curb Appeal

Start with the outside of your home. Many potential buyers drive by properties for sale before they ever make an appointment to see them. If your place isn't looking spiffy, buyers' interest may vaporize at first glance. Here's what to do for quick improvements:

- Trim scraggly bushes, shrubs, and trees.

- Plant attractive groups of annuals in bare spots, or to camouflage less than gorgeous views.

- A fresh coat of paint on exterior walls will do wonders.

- At least repaint trim, shutters, and the front door if they're looking tired or faded.

- Be sure windows are whole and that screens are in good shape.

- Have driveways, walkways, and concrete attended to if they're in disrepair.

- Inexpensive light fixtures can replace tarnished or discolored ones for a substantial cosmetic impact.

IF YOU'RE SO INCLINED

Drive around your neighborhood and see what draws your attention to other people's houses, then drive back to your own house and see what's different. It's a quick way to see your home through a prospective buyer's eyes!

While you're sprucing up the house, don't forget to do something for yourself too! This can be a stressful time, so treat yourself to fresh flowers to keep you smiling as you get things in order!

- Maybe the house needs a high-pressure hose washing to freshen it up.

- Be sure and put out a new welcome mat.

- Replace your house numbers if they're not great looking.

- Get rid of any piles of extra lumber, old flower pots, crumpled garbage cans, or dried up water hoses that you've been collecting for the last 20 years.

- Keep the walkways and sidewalks swept.

- Paint the lawn green. (I'm just checking to see if you're alert.)

Indoor Cosmetic Surgery

After the outside has been spiffed up, look at the inside of your home with new eyes. Better yet, ask a friend or realtor what they would suggest to create more sales appeal. The answer will undoubtedly be "less." Clearing the clutter is the single most important thing you can do to make your home look larger and more elegant. Here are some other things you might need to do:

- A coat of paint may be necessary to cover scratches, smears and fading.

- Replace worn carpeting.

- Install new vinyl flooring if yours is at all damaged or looks very dated.

- Scrub bathrooms and outfit them with new towels, throw rugs, and a shower curtain. (Remember, you can take the new purchases with you to your new house.) Hide all clutter and toiletries.

- Simple, but new and clean, curtains may be the ticket if you have old ones in bathrooms, bedrooms or in the kitchen.

- Buy new bedspreads and matching shams for an instant upgrade in bedrooms.

- Clear kitchen counters.

- A few plants and flowers, judiciously placed, can add an elegant touch.

- Be sure windows, mirrors and framed objects are gleaming.

- Straighten all hanging objects.

- Pick up everything off the floors.

- Pack some books and leave some bare space on shelves.

- Once again, be sure the tops of coffee tables, side tables, bathroom and kitchen counters, desks and bureaus are stripped down to the bare minimum. Anything left out in plain view should be attractive—not necessarily functional.

THE FINE ART OF DELEGATION. AGAIN.

If you're not up to the job of beautifying your house for sale, you should be aware that there are people who do this for a living. Called house stagers, they are

QUICK PAINLESS

Don't let it pile up! Once you've got the house spic 'n' span, set up a daily routine to keep it that way(get the whole family in on this one!) and that way you won't be caught off guard when a surprise potential buyer stops by!

Congratulations! You've made your house look its best! Treat yourself to a day at the salon and get in on the act!

The Lazy Way

experienced, and know what kinds of improvements have the most impact for the least amount of money. They also have the resources to quickly make significant changes. Ask local realtors for referrals. Some professional organizers do this type of work as well. (Ask for references, of course!)

Getting Time on Your Side

	The Old Way	The Lazy Way
Finding the directions to that office you went to last month	30 minutes	2 seconds
Buying the right fax paper for your machine	3 trips to the store	1 trip
Packing for a last-minute trip	2 hours	20 minutes
Getting your errands done	4 hours, once a week	30 minutes, twice a week
Giving someone your phone numbers	4 attempts	1 shot (with your card)
Paying the bills	An afternoon	30 minutes

Following Up with Cleaning Up

There is Basic Organizing, Organizing Intermediate, and then there's Organizing to the Max (or Organizing^2). If you've mastered the basics, here are some tricks to fine-tune your work. But feel free to snitch ideas from here if you like 'em, regardless of where you are on the organizational spectrum!

KEEP IT MOVING OUT OF YOUR LIFE: RECYCLING RESOURCES

If you've gotten in the habit of purging regularly—or even if you haven't—keep in mind that there are organizations willing to take some of your cast-offs out of your hands and put them to good use. Consider the following organizations in addition to the usual recipients of thrift stores, consignment shops, the garbage bin, and nonprofit organizations.

- Eyeglasses: LensCrafters has a "Give the Gift of Sight" program and will take your used glasses and distribute

QUICK ◉ PAINLESS

them to needy people all over the world. Call 800-522-LENS for a LensCrafters location.

- Computers: The obvious choice is local schools, churches, and nonprofit organizations.

  For a state-by-state directory of organizations that accept used computer equipment, log onto http://microweb.com/pepsite/Recycle/recycle_index.html.

- Another solution is the National Cristina Foundation, which will take your used equipment and give it to hospitals, job-training centers, and schools. Call 800-CRISTINA for information.

- Computer disks and CD-ROMs can be sent to CDIP Program, 5640 S. Durango, Tacoma, WA 98409. They grind up used disks and CDs to use in the manufacture of new computer products. Call GreenDisk at 800-305-DISK for information.

- Videotapes can be sent to ECO Media, 5429 La Palma Avenue, Anaheim Hills, CA 92807, or call 800-359-4601.

- Medicines (prescription and over-the-counter) and vitamins can be donated (after tossing expired ones) to MiraMed Institute, which sends medical supplies to Russian orphans. Call 800-441-1917 for information.

THE QUICKEST PATH TO CLEAN

Pros do it professionally, so use some of their tricks to make quick work of cleaning. Not all these ideas will apply to your particular situation, of course, but try out a few that look like improvements over your current cleaning routine.

- Keep cleaning supplies in several places so you can quickly mop up, sponge off, scrub, or dust while you're on the phone or whenever the mood strikes. Keep a set of the basics in each bathroom, for example. If you've got a two-story house, be sure and have a set of cleaning supplies on each floor.

- Gather all your cleaning equipment in a utility cart— the kind hotel housekeepers use. It should have a tray on top for cleaning supplies, and bins underneath to collect trash and dirty laundry. Wheel this cart from room to room systematically, plucking and dusting and clearing as you go. Follow that trip with a visit with the vacuum cleaner, and you're done.

- Do you feel overwhelmed by having to clean the whole house at once? Maybe it would be easier if you did one chore at a time. This could mean setting aside one day to just do floors or polish all the wood furniture or take down drapes for cleaning and launder any washable curtains in the house.

- Another approach is to clean one room at a time. However you do it is perfectly acceptable.

A CLEANING PRIMER

Here are some basic techniques to use if you're the one cleaning your house:

IF YOU'RE SO INCLINED

If finances allow, hire regular cleaning help. If that's not doable, hire someone to do just the big jobs: windows, the basement, or the kitchen a few times a year. Individuals are good; cleaning services who arrive with a team of workers and leave a few hours later with everything clean at once are the greatest.

When cleaning, start at the top! That way you can do everything just once, instead of having to sweep all over again every time you start working on a new surface!

- Start at the top. Dust from the top down so that settling debris gets picked up eventually by the vacuum cleaner.

- Walls are next: Don't forget to dust door frames and picture frames. Fingerprints around light switches and doors get wiped out with an all-purpose cleaner. A particularly smeary window might need cleaning, and most mirrors will need a weekly swipe with glass cleaner.

- Then furniture: Dust first. Polish wood furniture every once in a while (or when it starts looking dull). Spot-clean upholstery where needed. Fluff up pillows.

- Last of all is vacuuming: first, the backs and bottoms of upholstery, and then the floors.

SHOPPING WITHOUT EVER STEPPING INTO A STORE

Many resources are available these days to help you cut your shopping time. Use technology and some new personal-service businesses to bring you what you need, when you need it, on *your* time schedule. In most cases, you pay a shipping charge, but weigh the cost of that charge against your time, use of the car, and your limited energy reserves depleted by cruising the malls. Not to mention that it's a lot harder to do impulse shopping on the telephone or online.

Fast Food

- Order your groceries by phone or fax. Some larger chains have e-mail ordering services; you can pick up your groceries, or they sometimes deliver. Smaller, independent grocers sometimes offer fax-in order services. You fax your grocery list to them; they pluck and pack; you pick up. Worth a try!

- A national source is NetGrocer, found online at www5.netgrocer.com. Shop any time of day, pick your groceries from a full range of choices, and pay $2.99 shipping for orders up to $50 and $4.99 for all orders above $50. Your order arrives within one to four days by Federal Express. Check it out!

- It's becoming less and less common, but try to get your milk home-delivered. Call around to local dairies and see if one provides this service. Getting your milk and other dairy products delivered will, I guarantee, have a tremendous time- and money-saving impact. You won't need to visit the grocery store nearly as often as before, and you will definitely buy less food.

- If cooking is not your thing, or lack of time makes it impossible, ask friends or neighbors if they know of any local frozen-food purveyors. You can get high quality and tremendous convenience with home-delivered, prepared food products. These services can make your life a lot easier.

- Check your local Yellow Pages for organizations that will deliver groceries and other food items to your

A COMPLETE WASTE OF TIME

The 3 worst Things You Can Do When it Comes to Your Grocery Shopping Are:

1. Do it in multiple trips

2. Don't keep a list going

3. Don't try grocery delivery services

home. They'll save you loads of time otherwise spent at the supermarket, and their prices are usually very competitive!

CLOTHING

Clothes can be purchased in several ways other than trips to the mall or a trek downtown. Use the telephone to call department stores and place a phone order for an advertised item. A credit card number is all you need. Catalogs are great time-savers, and you can shop any time of the day or night. Online shopping from your favorite catalog sources is also extremely convenient.

Direct sales is an increasingly popular way to shop for women's clothing. You can see samples of the clothes you order and get, for no additional charge, the services of a knowledgeable consultant who can advise you on putting together a wardrobe and getting the proper fit. Companies such as Doncaster offer their own line of high-quality clothes that you can purchase in a one-hour appointment in the home or studio of one of their consultants. Visit Doncaster's Web site at http://www.Doncaster.com.

Cosmetics and skin care products can also be purchased conveniently at a representative's home or from one of their catalogs. Companies such as Mary Kay and Avon offer fine products, individual attention, and absolutely no trips to the store. Call 800/598-1069 to find a local Mary Kay rep and 800/735-8867 for the nearest Avon lady near you.

YOUR LIFE IN BOOK FORM

Another way to keep track of your life is by consolidating all important information on paper into a binder. This is a binder you can keep separate from or add to your "Important Papers" Binder, mentioned in Chapter 7. And you don't have to duplicate information you will put into your "End of Life" binder discussed next.

You can make your own version of your life binder, or you can purchase one already organized for you. A particularly good one is the At-A-Glance's LifeLinks Family Central binder. Not only is it attractive, but it has a wealth of blank 8 1/2" x 11" preprinted forms which prompt you to fill them out.

Included in the LifeLink system are tabs labeled Family, Finances, Home, Activities, Addresses and Miscellaneous. If you'd like to make your own binder, here's what to include, following the Family Central arrangement:

- Under the Family tab, you'll find Personal Data forms that are meant to be filled out for each family member. They call for the obvious like birth date and birthplace, but also ask for social security number, blood type, allergies, and a place to note medical and dental histories and immunizations. Still under the family section, you'll find a form to be filled out for the babysitter and some simple life-saving diagrams and instructions. There's a form for "Elder Information," on which you can list your senior's doctors, medications, insurance information and the locations of their will, health care proxy and power of attorney. Even the family pet has a page on which to record visits to the vet!

- The Finance section includes listings for checking, savings, money market and CD accounts, credit card numbers (with their phone numbers!), monthly bills and account numbers, insurance policy numbers and expiration dates, and budgeting forms.

- Under Home, you'll find a page on which you enter the names and numbers of your maintenance resources: the plumber, electrician, and painter, to name a few. Under each name is a space to write what needs to be done next time that person has to make a visit. Brilliant idea! There is also a form listing service records for your large appliances—the stove, air conditioning unit, computers, etc. And a "Record of Improvements"—both interior and exterior—will help you remember who did what where. Last, but not least, there is a page for every month of the year listing appropriate things to be done around the house that month.

- The Activities section lists kids' activities, coaches, times, and contact telephone numbers. (I'd add my kids' rosters to this part of the binder). There's also a place to list some school information, like the principal's name and bus number, your child's classroom number, and teacher's name and number. There are also handy forms here to list greeting cards sent, presents given, a birthday list, and a vacation planning form.

QUICK ⚉ PAINLESS

At the first of every year, go through your binders and update them. This way, you'll never get behind and always have relevant information available to you.

- The Address section is self-explanatory (but has all emergency numbers on the first page), and Miscellaneous is just that—you put in everything you think important but don't know how to classify.

Think what a boon to have a binder like this filled out and updated regularly!

GETTING THE END OF YOUR LIFE IN ORDER

One of the most significant organizing tasks you can do is to get your affairs in order in preparation for your own disability or death. It's not morbid, really, but a practical thing to do, and the kindest gift you can give to your caregivers and survivors.

- Should you get sick and unable to care for yourself, get things in place so your caregivers can do the best job possible.

- Even if you've expressed your wishes verbally, there is nothing as good as having something in writing regarding your wishes for medical treatment, your belongings, and who you want in charge. Make those decisions now. You can always change your mind.

- I had a client not too long ago, the father of a friend of mine. He hired me to help him go through a lifetime of papers, records, and documents, explaining that he'd rather pay me and participate himself now than leave the task to his daughter some day. What a thoughtful man.

QUICK PAINLESS

I just discovered what looks to be a wonderful aid to people with chronic or catastrophic illness. A young woman, who underwent a life-saving heart transplant, and her husband created a "Personal Health-Care Organizer," a binder that serves as a history, journal, and guide for patients and their caregivers. It holds forms to be filled in as treatments are followed, records information needed in emergency situations, and tracks medications and insurance information. Call 800-708-7623 for information, or log onto www.andreas.com/crakel.

WHO NEEDS TO KNOW WHAT

Your relatives, upon your death, should be prepared ahead of time by knowing your wishes and where to find everything they need. The easiest way to do this is prepare a binder containing all the information they might need. Spend some time gathering and writing down the following information on eight different lists:

1. Make a list naming and giving telephone numbers of your:

   - Family members
   - CPA
   - Employer (your supervisor and secretary)
   - Stockbroker
   - Doctors
   - Lawyer
   - Banker
   - Financial adviser
   - Minister or priest
   - Executor of your estate or trustee of your trust

2. Make another list of the following types of numbers:

   - Social Security number
   - Health insurance certificate
   - All bank and credit union accounts
   - Safe-deposit box (and location of keys)

YOU'LL THANK YOURSELF LATER

Red Alert: Do not store the only copy of this information in your safe-deposit box. Often these boxes are sealed upon the holder's death!

- Pension and retirement sources
- Mortgage holder
- Investment accounts
- Driver's license
- Passport number
- All credit cards (make a photocopy of both fronts and backs)

3. A third section should alert readers to the existence and location of your "Important Papers" binder (see Chapter 7, "Turn Paper Piles into Efficient Files").

4. The fourth list should note the location of what's filed away that others will need to know about. This may include:

- Current tax information
- Past tax returns
- Real estate deeds
- Employment records
- Deed to your home and other real estate
- Bank passbooks
- Stock certificates, savings bonds, and certificates of deposit

5. Insurance policies should be another list; include policy numbers, the location of each policy, and names and telephone numbers of all insurance agents.

IF YOU'RE SO
INCLINED

Be sure to authorize one person to share your safe-deposit box with you. You don't need to give this person a key, but let her know where she can find one upon your death. She doesn't need access to the box while you're alive, but will be able to retrieve it after you're gone.

6. Make a list of your personal property and include:

   ▪ Information about each vehicle you own and location of deeds of ownership

   ▪ Jewelry, collections, and art

   ▪ Appraisals of valuable property

7. Make a note of any loans that are due you and a list of any major outstanding debts or loans you owe (aside from routine monthly bills).

8. Create a list of all monthly income and expenses so that your survivors will know what to expect.

Be sure your will lists how you want your personal belongings distributed. If you've promised specific items to specific people, be sure to write that down, too.

If you have minor children, make sure you have written plans for their care and education.

More Words on Your "Important Papers" Binder

Have a file or section of your binder devoted to your written funeral information and wishes:

▪ Any prepaid or preplanned arrangements.

▪ Choice of mortuary and/or cemetery.

▪ Deed of cemetery plot.

▪ Memorial or burial service wishes (include music, who you'd like to participate, and what you'd like read or recited).

Another tool available to buy, if you're not making your own End of Life binder, is a binder made by Active Insights. It's called "The Beneficiary Book: A Family Information Organizer," and is somewhat of a hybrid between a Life, End of Life, and Important Papers binder. Its forms are unique in that they are printed with a series of questions that, when answered, will result in a complete workbook of all your family's information.

Get yourself some help pulling this information together. Once you get started, it's not as daunting a task as it looks on paper. Make a reminder to yourself to look through your binder at the beginning of every year to update or make changes or corrections. And know that nothing you do will be as helpful to the people who love you as getting this information together for them.

Congratulations! You've gotten the end of your life in order! Now spend today with the people you love and have some fun!

The Lazy Way

Getting Time on Your Side

	The Old Way	The Lazy Way
Doing a cleaning "quick pass"	An afternoon	1 hour
Getting the groceries	2 hours	They're delivered!
Buying a gift at the mall	An afternoon	A few minutes on the phone
Finding the number of your accountant	An hour leafing through files	2 seconds! (It's on a list!)
Figuring out what to do with the stuff you don't need	Possibly never	A few quick calls
Making sure your estate is in order	What?! Now?	30 minutes, once a year

The Room-by-Room Treatment Plan

Are you too lazy to read The Room-by -Room Treatment Plan?

1 You love your desk, but you can't work at it any longer—it's covered with paper. ☐ yes ☐ no

2 The children left years ago, but you can't move to a smaller place because you have so much "stuff." ☐ yes ☐ no

3 Does your idea of "throwing out" mean moving things into the garage? ☐ yes ☐ no

Getting the Home Office Up to Speed

You don't need a job with a paycheck to earn the right to a workspace. The business of life is a full-time job. If you pay bills, rent or own a home, belong to a club, talk on the telephone, or have children, you've got a job whether you like it or not. Making fast work of routine chores is the secret to getting—and staying—organized.

You may have a smooth-running office at the office, but fall down on the business part of your private life. Here's how to set up a space to get it organized. Don't forget that these ideas can be taken out of the house to an office anywhere.

An office—base camp, so to speak—that acts as the single hub where all the business of your life gets processed is the key to good organization. This is where mail should end up, as well as kids' papers, bills, forms to fill out, and anything else that requires action or represents a business function of your work or home life.

A PLACE TO CALL YOUR OWN

Where to start? Begin by canvassing your home for a space you can call your own. No hard hat required. It can be as small as a corner under a stairway or as big as a whole room. You might need to make some sacrifices to accommodate your need for a workspace. Do it! As you will see later, this office space can be the center of your operations and is a crucial foundation for your new organized life.

Here are some suggestions for office space:

- Guest room: If it's used three times a year and you need an office 250 days a year, rethink your space priorities! A small workspace might easily fit into or replace the guest room.

- Bedrooms can often serve double duty if you remove unused furniture (when did you last sit in that rocking chair or use that treadmill?) and think creatively to accommodate a work area and file cabinet. Even a card table, covered with a cloth, can store a file box and function as a work surface in the bedroom.

- The double closet with standard sliding doors in your guest room, exercise room, or even your bedroom can be a great office. Remove the doors and build in or place a desk along the closet's back wall, or use folding louver doors that can be pushed shut to hide your work area. A decorative screen would serve the same purpose.

- Under a stairway: You'll need good lighting if it's within the stairwell (unless you enjoy wearing that miner's hat with a light on top), and you may need to stoop a bit to get into a sitting position, but if it's all you've got, it will work just fine.

- Less desirable, but possible, is a corner or length of countertop in the kitchen. The kitchen is usually such a busy place; it lacks privacy and quiet, and it's easy to mix up Ragu with receipts and fettuccini with files. But if it's your only alternative, carve out a spot for yourself. Find some room in a cupboard to stash work so that it's secure and out of sight—and out of range of splattering salsa.

- If your family room is large enough, a corner might be turned into a work area.

- Living rooms are generally left pristine and unused. Set up an attractive work area and get your real estate working for you!

Tools of the Trade

You wouldn't expect an auto mechanic to do his job without a toolbox. Likewise, you need the right tools to do your job efficiently. Make sure you're equipped to do that job properly.

Whatever space you end up with, you need to accommodate several essentials. The first is as large a desk as you can fit in your space. There are many alternatives:

- A standard office variety.

- A sleek contemporary job.

YOU'LL THANK YOURSELF LATER

Establishing a place to process paper is without a doubt one of the most important steps you can take to get organized. Making your space as attractive and functional as possible—this means investing in good furniture and equipment—will pay huge dividends in the future.

- A built-in counter.

- A table.

- A door-sized board placed on top of two, two-drawer file cabinets.

- L-shaped and parallel desks work really well. They make it possible for you to sit in one spot and be able to reach most things without getting up—a real time-saver.

- If your workspace is highly visible, look for a rolltop desk or one that has a flip-up work counter. They function as both workspace and hiding place in one.

- Aim for the most workspace inches you can eke out.

- Drawers are essential for keeping office supplies close at hand; try to get a desk that has one or two.

- Traditional desks have a file drawer in them, which is great for keeping your most important, or most used, papers accessible.

Climbing the Walls Again

The next item you're going to need is shelves, as many as you can get. You simply can't have too much shelving. You can buy the components at a home building store and install them yourself, or get a handyperson to build them. Or buy or build bookcases.

If you have wall space above your desk, build shelves above it, using the whole width (and height) your space allows. Put the lowest shelf very low—within arm's length while you are sitting down at your desk—so that

QUICK PAINLESS

If you use the phone a lot, treat yourself to a real shoulder and neck-saver: a telephone headset. There are many styles available from Hello Direct, as well as office supply stores. You will find that your neck stays flexible and your arms and hands are free to keep doing whatever they were doing when the telephone rang.

you can easily reach the things placed on it. The idea is to keep your desk clear for work and not have to get up and walk across the room for frequently used items. For example, on the shelf closest to you, place your phone book, the stapler, and your binder of lists.

If there's no way to get a shelf above your desk area, place a bookcase or two (as large as will fit) as close to your desk as possible.

Be sure that your shelves are deep enough to hold a binder—approximately 12 inches deep.

The Telephone and Swell Accessories

Another essential is—brrrnggg—a telephone. There is no way to efficiently conduct business in your office with your telephone in another room. Bite the bullet and get your space wired to the outside world.

Here are some add-ons to consider that will make your life easier:

- An answering machine
- A voicemail system
- A fax machine

The File Cabinet

More office basics: the file cabinet. Place at least one close to your desk and set it up using the system you will learn by heart in chapter 7 called, funnily enough, "Turn Paper Piles into Efficient Files." Be sure to get a good-quality file cabinet, and consider both regular cabinets and lateral ones. More about these issues in the paper and filing chapter, too.

IF YOU'RE SO INCLINED

Consider installing a second telephone line to use as a dedicated fax line. If your telephone and fax machines share the same line, people are obliged to call you to ask that you turn it on before they can fax you. The idea is to avoid conversations, not have extra ones. A second telephone line can also be used for your computer modem so that you can send and retrieve faxes and e-mail as well as access the Internet without tying up your phone line.

Let There Be Light

Good lighting is another essential. The following list should shed some light on this important item:

- Overhead light combined with a task light (a lamp that illuminates the work area on your desk) is the best solution.

- You don't have to use official "office" light fixtures. Be creative: Use any lamp that is attractive and illuminates well, even if it's meant for the living room or bedroom.

- If you're doing this on the cheap, look at office supply stores for clamp-on, swing-arm task lamps. (They also save space.)

Have a Seat

A good chair is another item you don't want to economize on, especially if you spend long hours in front of the computer. Your fanny and back are worth buying the best for, and you'll be less likely to experience back, shoulder, and neck pain with the right support. The chair's back and seat should be adjustable, so that your thighs are parallel to the floor when your feet are resting flat on the floor. You should also feel your lower back being supported.

- You want comfort and ergonomically correct support to protect your back. Office supply stores have a great selection.

- Get the best you can afford.

QUICK ☜🎀☞ PAINLESS

A plastic floor mat is not only fun to slide around on, but essential if you have carpeting so you can quickly scoot from one workspace to another or swivel around from one side of your desk to the other. Mats used on carpeting have short, sharp teeth that grip the carpet and prevent the mat from sliding around. You can also get mats to protect hard floor surfaces.

No arms—they can get in the way or even pinch your fingers when you open a drawer or turn your chair.

The Small Stuff

A few drawers for storing small stuff are handy. If your desk doesn't have drawers, try a small cabinet or cupboard. Office supplies can go into baskets or bins and be placed out of the way in the drawers or on shelves. Rolling carts with swing-out drawers can also do the job and be pushed out of the way when not needed.

THE TRIED AND TRUE DESK SETUP

Here's a great way to set up your desk: It works for me and it works for many of my clients. By eliminating clutter and keeping just the essentials up and handy, you should be able to have more work room, concentrate on the tasks at hand, find it easier to keep things cleared off, and work comfortably.

Start by arranging the telephone, the computer if you use one, a lamp, and a small collection of upright file folders (see the chapter on paper and filing).

- Put your computer monitor up on a swivel-arm platform, freeing up desk space.

- Use one receptacle for pens and pencils; stash the rest in a drawer or cupboard.

- Keep clutter to a minimum; stash small items in the closest drawer.

Whatever you do, make your workspace as attractive as possible, a place you don't mind hanging out in for a short while every day or most days of the week. Paint the walls and hang your favorite artwork on them. Hang curtains or drapes if you need them. Wash the windows. Add a plant or fresh flowers. A few— a very few—personal items can join you. Make it bright, make it cheery, but don't clutter it.

The Lazy Way

◼ Don't forget to use the shelf above your desk—if you have one—to keep the other most-used items you need handy.

MORE OFFICE TIPS

Stacking trays are good for keeping different sorts and colors of blank paper (your letterhead, second sheets, and copy paper, for example) and blank forms in order.

On shelves, place your binders, each of which holds a project or group of like documents, such as rosters or CDs. Label each binder in large, bold letters—no squinting allowed.

Magazines, the very few you have decided to hang on to, go into "magazine butlers," those great boxes that hold magazines and can be labeled; they hold their contents upright, out of sight yet accessible. You can find every type, from chic woven ones to see-through plastic styles to inexpensive flat cardboard ones that can be folded into boxes. They also hold bulky materials, such as catalogs or computer manuals, together.

Use see-through plastic envelopes to hold papers belonging together. You can find the envelopes in letter and legal sizes, and they organize projects wonderfully.

A High-Tech Note

The telephone and fax are the two most basic tools, but you can go much, much further with the technology available today. An obvious example is the computer. This is not the book to deal with setting up computer systems. However, I'll be covering a number of computer-friendly solutions to organizing. One option for your office is an all-in-one machine that combines a plain-paper fax, copier, scanner, and black-and-white or color printer for your computer.

If you use your computer a lot, consider wrist-rests to help prevent carpal tunnel syndrome.

Just the Fax

Why a fax machine, you ask? A fax sends and receives information without a conversation. I'm not against talking, mind you, and it's vitally important to connect with your customers or children or the plumber. But the simple truth is that the fewer conversations you engage in, the more time you're going to save. And the more meaningless conversations you skip, the more meaningful conversations you can fit into your life!

Faxes cut down on not only telephone conversations, but also your outgoing mail. There are many occasions when using the fax makes sense and saves time and money:

- Ask people to fax you information instead of taking it over the telephone. You'll save time.

- You'll end up with a written copy of what was sent, so there can't be any mistakes.

- Faxes don't require preliminaries to conversations such as, "How are you?" and hearing about someone's bad cold or bad commute, unrelated to the matter at hand.

- If others need information from you, fax it.

IF YOU'RE SO INCLINED

If you've got a computer, and you don't yet have e-mail, get a modem and immediately lunge for the phone and sign up with a service provider. It will not always replace the fax machine, but just about. And it's instant and cheap. You'll need a telephone line, which is just another good reason to have a second line in your office. With only one telephone line, people calling you get an annoying busy signal while you're on the Internet.

- You can fax after normal business hours when telephone rates are cheaper and when it may be more convenient for you.

- Leave your fax number as part of your message on your answering machine, suggesting that callers fax what they have to say.

- Fax your clients or business associates to confirm appointments.

- Fax the drugstore for prescription refills.

- Send letters or invoices by fax, saving paper, postage, and time.

- If you don't use the Internet for this purpose, place catalog orders to those companies with fax order numbers. You can do this any time, night or day.

Incidentally, there are some ways to streamline even faxing:

- You don't have to type everything you fax; neatly handwritten notes are fine.

- You'll waste a lot of paper and transmission time using a whole sheet as a cover page. Either use a sticky note with the notation "three-page fax to Debbie," or type or write the same thing on the top of your letter you are faxing.

- 3M makes a Post-It header note just for faxes.

- If you want quick and you want easy, using the fax regularly is one of the best habits you can get into.

YOU'LL THANK YOURSELF LATER

Most fax machines use thermal paper that comes on rolls. More expensive initially, but possibly worth it to you, would be a plain-paper fax. This way you'll avoid curlicues of faxes snaking all over your desk as you receive faxes and you won't need to make copies of them.

THE OL' ROUTINE

Now that you have an office, what do you do in there? All the equipment and systems in the world aren't going to do you any good if you don't make a pact with yourself to use them. You start by taking small steps—every day.

- Mail needs to come directly to the office. Do not pass go, do not collect anything on the way.

- Become best friends with the wastepaper basket. Stand over it while you open your mail.

- Use your upright files to take care of the majority of mail you keep. (See the chapter on paper and filing.)

- No need to open the bills before tossing them in the "Bills to Pay" folder (unless you've loaned your credit cards to your kids).

- Pay your bills only once or twice a month. Writing checks as bills come in, plus stamping, addressing, and mailing them, is a big time-waster.

- Just get the stuff off piles and into files. This is truly a feel-good exercise!

KEEPING TRACK OF EVERYONE IN YOUR LIFE

Addresses and telephone numbers can be a real hassle these days. It seems as though everyone is continually on the move, or their area codes have been changed, or they're getting e-mail addresses. Here are some ways to keep track of everyone:

A COMPLETE WASTE OF TIME

The 3 Worst Ways to Use a Fax:

1. To send thank you letters.

2. To express apologies or condolences.

3. In the middle of the night to those with home offices whose fax machine is in the bedroom. Try to determine where people's fax machines are located before sending midnight faxes!

- A Rolodex, with cards that can be deleted and inserted into the system. (Don't put plastic covers over each card. You'll have to remove the card from the cover to jot changes and additions to your entries.) You can buy different-colored refill cards, however. Use one color for personal entries and another for business, or use one color for parents' numbers and another one for children.

- A handwritten address book. Write in pencil and erase to make changes.

- A computer-generated address book. I find this last alternative the most efficient, and it works great if you are computer-savvy.

Whichever system you choose, be scrupulous about updating your information as you receive it, and you won't need to hang on to all those little scraps of paper that accumulate on your desk. I've seen clients with piles of opened envelopes sitting around with return addresses on them waiting to be noted somewhere. Do it now!

Your Address Book: So Much More Than Addresses

Use your address book for much more than a record of names and addresses. It can be a valuable repository of a wealth of information:

- Your children's and spouse's Social Security numbers, allergies, sizes, and color preferences.

- Bank account numbers.

- Health insurance certificate numbers.

- The numbers of often-filled prescription can go next to the pharmacist's telephone number.
- Driver's license numbers.

TAKING CHARGE OF THE PHONE

One of the best ways to manage your time is to control the telephone instead of letting it control you.

If you're in the middle of a project or important conversation, don't answer the telephone. Let the answering machine or your voicemail system fill in for you. This takes self-discipline, but you will increase your productivity by not allowing interruptions and by concentrating on the task at hand. Then, when you're ready to return calls, go through your messages and return them by importance to you—not to the caller.

Professional Protocol

When you reach an answering machine, leave a real message stating the purpose of your call, instead of just asking to be called back. Be concise and leave all the information someone needs to act or to answer you. The telephone tag game will be a lot shorter. I can't overemphasize that you should always speak slowly and clearly when leaving messages, especially if you're calling someone who doesn't know you. Your name or company name spoken in one syllable is most likely unintelligible. Slow down! And always give your return number at both the beginning and end of your message. You might also suggest what times you are most likely to be available to

QUICK ☎ PAINLESS

Write down all your telephone messages either in an NCR telephone message pad, so that you always have a copy of it, or a small spiral-bound notebook. That way, all your notes and information will be in your message pad or notebook should you ever have to go back and find a number or information you jotted down during a call.

increase your chances of connecting. (I know you're busy but, no, you may not suggest 3 A.M. as the only sure time to find you available.)

If you run a business, make a form for information gathering, including name, address and all phone numbers, but also who referred them to you, and so on. This form acts as a prompt to collect all the information you need on the first phone call, instead of having to call back with "Which product did you say you were interested in?" or "How many employees did you say you had?" You can file these forms in a folder or binder for future reference and as a good tracking device.

Getting Time on Your Side

	The Old Way	**The Lazy Way**
Finding an important phone number	An afternoon	2 seconds
Getting in touch with someone	A week	1 day
Finding an article on bee-keeping that you tore out to read	17 minutes because it's buried in a pile	17 seconds in your bee-keeping file folder
Doing a half-hour project	65 minutes over 3 days because of telephone interruptions	35 minutes in one sitting (by ignoring the telephone)
Distributing a meeting agenda to five people	45 minutes	10 minutes (using the fax machine)
Filling out a form requiring birth date, Social Security number, and driver's license number	17 minutes	5 minutes (all information is in your address book)

Turn Paper Piles into Efficient Files

Feel like you're drowning in paper? You're not alone. Paper is overwhelming us. It comes from all directions, it comes in duplicate and triplicate, and it arrives daily. Notice you haven't heard anyone talk about "the paperless society" recently? There's a reason for that. Computers, as wonderful as they are, have increased our paper production and consumption. Now everyone gets a copy. Now you can make last-minute changes and reprint. Now you can fax a copy and send a hard copy. Now you can be knee-deep in paper within a week.

Keeping up with the flow is tough, but very doable once you have a system in place to manage it. (And, of course, the self-discipline to keep up the system.) By now, I hope you've set up a space for working, complete with a desk, a chair, and a file cabinet. Here's why you set all that up:

One of life's major mysteries might be what to keep and what to toss. Keep reading for the elusive answer to this question. I'm going to walk you through a couple of *Lazy Way* systems of keeping paper, encourage you to throw out a lot of paper that you don't need, and then set up a filing system to make quick work of archiving what paper you keep. Then I'll show you how to go back into ancient history and your piles or boxes of old stuff. You'll be ready to purge and merge and file what's important at warp speed.

FIGHTING THE GOOD FIGHT: THE WAR ON PAPER

You can start with today's mail. The absolute first thing you do with the mail is throw out everything you can before it even gets into the house. Be sure you have a large wastepaper basket wherever the mail makes its entrance. You know at a glance whether offers for new credit cards, new magazine subscriptions, or solicitations for donations are relevant to you. If you have no intention of applying, acquiring, or donating, don't even open the envelope. Out it goes. The same rule applies to all other junk mail.

Use caution, of course. If you're at all in doubt, be sure to open the envelope to scan its contents. Occasionally—direct mail designers being as clever as they are—you open envelopes you were sure contained a check or something equally important and are disappointed. But better to have checked. If it's a reject, be sure it hits the trashcan immediately.

Throwing out mail at the point of entry does more to streamline your paper problems than anything else.

Now What?

Step Two: What's left after you've tossed the junk? Most likely bills, personal correspondence (on a good day), and the great assorted mishmash that ends up in piles or boxes and makes you crazy because you don't know what to do with it. Here's how to handle this stuff.

There are two places your paper should end up: on your desktop file system or in your file cabinet. We'll tackle the desktop first and deal with the file cabinet later in this chapter.

THE DESKTOP FILE SYSTEM

Once you've become used to this arrangement, there's no going back. My clients love this system and you will, too.

Desktop filing consists of putting the six to ten most-used files you need on the top of your desk, upright and visible. (*Upright* is the operative word here.) These are files you need, if not every day, at least several times a week. After throwing out what you can of the day's mail, you make a quick transition to your desktop and distribute the mail into these folders. It gets housed immediately, it does not sit in piles, and it does not get lost.

The Crucial Piece

To set up your desktop file system, get a small filing box or frame that holds hanging folders upright. The manila files you make for your desktop get put into the hanging folders. Or use metal or plastic interlocking holders. You don't use hanging folders for this type; just stick your

IF YOU'RE SO INCLINED

Throwing out junk mail is dealing with the symptom, not the disease. Start with the source and cut out junk mail. Here's how to eliminate at least 25 percent of it: Write to the Mail Preference Service, Direct Marketing Association, 11 W. 42nd Street, New York, NY 10163-3861. Request that they remove your name from their direct mail lists. (You have to resend this letter every year or so, but it still saves you time.)

files into them. The one I use most often is the Eldon Add-A-File. You can add and subtract partitions depending on how many files you need.

File Folder Finesse

Then make your manila file folders. Buy "third cut" files. They have tabs that are one third the length of the folder, giving you plenty of room to write. Then mark your files clearly and in big letters. Legibility is the key. Write right on the paper tab; save labels for re-using your folders.

The Desktop Design

What's absolutely essential is that (a) your folders are upright, facing you, well within easy reach, and that (b) you mark your folders clearly, in big, bold letters so you can see all your desktop folders at a glance.

The Most-Wanted List

The files on your desktop usually include the following:

- **Bills to Pay.** You don't even have to open these envelopes; just toss them in. If you choose to open your bills, make sure you toss all the inserts that come with them. You should end up with one bill and one envelope. I paper clip them so they stay together.

- **To Be Filed.** Anything that does not require action, but that needs to be saved, goes in here if you don't have the time to file it immediately.

QUICK ◼ PAINLESS

Make separate folders for all those things you do at least once a week for your desktop, and stop having to hunt around each time you need something!

- Any other subject you use often. You probably have at least one person you pass things on to regularly, so make a folder for that person.

- Why not make one for your spouse? That way, things he or she needs to review have a home, instead of sitting around getting lost in a pile.

- Do you regularly send clippings to your best friend? Make a folder with his or her name on it.

- Do you often cut out recipes at your desk? Make a folder to hold them until you can file or get them into the kitchen.

- Then, make one for the super-wonderful, how-did-you-ever-live-without-it **Pending** folder.

The Pending File

This is a handy invention—not to be confused with your whole life, which is, of course, "pending"! In this case, *pending* means short-term items that will be resolved within a few weeks. Here are some suggestions on what you can put into your pending folder:

- Invitations (after you've noted the date in your calendar), because they often tell you details such as the dress code or directions to the event.

- The page from a mail order catalog showing what you ordered, on which you have jotted the order date and order number.

- Pending health insurance claims.

- Tickets to upcoming events.

A COMPLETE WASTE OF TIME

The 3 Three Worst Things to Do When Filing:

1. Use paper clips to permanently hold things together. They get caught up on each other and use a lot of space. Staple stuff that needs to stay together.

2. File papers in the back of the folder. You want to see the latest first, generally, so file the most recent papers in the front of the folder.

3. Wait too long to file. The longer you wait, the more onerous the task seems. Do a little every day. Remember, it's much easier to keep up than catch up!

- The agenda for next week's meeting.
- Tickets and itinerary for the trip you're about to take.
- Your sample ballot if it's election time.
- A copy of miscellaneous letters you're expecting a quick reply to.

Once a week or so, go through your pending folder. You'll probably find several pieces of paper that have already been handled and can be tossed or filed. This is a great place to park things that are in a holding pattern, and it sure beats having them buried under a stack of papers on your desk somewhere!

PANDORA'S BOX TO PERFECTION

Now for the file cabinet. You may hate filing. You might not even own a file cabinet. But if you get one and use it, it will be the answer to "Now what do I do with THIS?" many, many times. Be sure your file cabinet has rods for hanging folders, or place wire racks in the file drawer to hold them. Hanging folders are the secret to finding things easily in your file cabinet, so they are absolutely essential.

Whether you use a letter- or legal-sized file cabinet depends on what you're storing. If you have a lot of legal or real estate documents, you're probably better off with the wider size. Otherwise, letter size works for most folks.

Use the same type manila file folders that you created for your desktop, and mark them the same way.

The reasoning behind filing is pretty simple. There are two basic motives for saving paper. The first is crucial:

YOU'LL THANK YOURSELF LATER

Buy the best filing cabinet you can afford. Cheap ones can be hard to open, don't glide easily, fall off their tracks, and lose their handles. You want to make filing as easy and pleasant as possible— not fight with a piece of furniture.

preparing your income taxes and proving your expenses and income to the Internal Revenue Service. How you set up a filing system is determined by your tax situation. Depending on whether you're a homeowner or a renter, self-employed or an employee, and other variables, you'll have different needs from your filing system.

The second reason is to save stuff is for sentimental reasons. Everything else is strictly optional or needs to be kept for just a short time.

The list of subjects below covers tax-related items, things you need to track for at least a few months (like your credit card bills), and sentimental-type papers. If you're setting up a system for your home and family (and every home and family needs a system, believe me!), your folders might be labeled as follows:

- **Medical Insurance**

- **Life and/or Disability Insurance**

- **Medical Bills Paid**

- **Utilities,** maybe all together. You probably don't need to keep all of them. We'll discuss bill paying and purging files later.

- **Mortgage**

- **Bank Statements.** Unfold them, place them in a folder, remove the canceled checks, and store them in a box. Make a file for each bank account you have.

- **Credit Cards,** a separate folder for each card. Drop in your charge receipts as you get them.

Remember that there is no one right way to set up a filing system. If you can find what you've filed 3 weeks after you've filed it, you've done a superb job! Get yourself a plant or poster for your office.

The Lazy Way

Credit Card Offers. If you occasionally switch credit cards to get lower interest rates, this folder is where you collect credit card offers.

Auto, which could include all your vehicles or a folder for each vehicle. These files may include insurance policies and information, or you might choose to make separate auto insurance files. Pink slips, service records, and registration documents all go into your vehicle folder(s).

Taxes (current year). As things accumulate that don't fit into other categories, pop them in here. Tax articles, notices, and other miscellaneous items you think might be relevant to preparing your tax returns can go into this folder.

Taxes (prior years). You might keep the past 2 to 5 years handy in your file cabinet.

Property Taxes

Investments, usually one folder per account.

Charities or **Donations,** if you collect a lot of receipts during the year. (If you just have a few, put them in this year's tax folder.)

Instructions and **Warranties** (for all the stuff you own).

Pets

If you're a homeowner, make a folder marked **Home Improvements.** Use it for all receipts for major or semi-permanent improvements made to your home. Hang on to your Home Improvements file as long as you own your home. The information in the folder will affect your tax situation when you sell your house. Ask your tax preparer exactly what types of improvements you need to track.

- Make a folder for **Each Child.** Into it, put their medical records, letters they've sent you, test scores, or anything special that might not end up in their school papers envelope. (See Chapter 12, "Kids and Clean-Up: It Can Be Done!")

Then, the folders of a more personal nature get established. They vary according to your interests, hobbies, or business and may include the following:

- **Travel,** for where you've been or where you're going, articles, and brochures.

- **Correspondence To Answer,** where letters can sit in a holding pattern until you answer them.

- **Correspondence To Save**

- Make a folder with **Your Name** on it for just personal stuff: your tarot card reading or an award or fan mail or for something you have no idea what to do with.

- Make a folder for **Each Organization** you belong to for collecting their newsletters and other information.

- Maybe you need one for **Articles To Read,** which are just articles that have been cut out of newspapers or magazines.

- **Recipes**

YOU'LL THANK YOURSELF LATER

By making a folder for all the recurring events in your life, you'll save yourself oodles of time each week by starting out organized, instead trying to play catch up!

■ **Garden Ideas** or **House Ideas**

■ If you're self-employed, make a folder called **Cash Receipts.** This folder is for purchases that you did not charge or write a check for.

Only you can know what categories you need folders for, but you should have one for every area of your life that involves paper you hang on to. And if you see a folder on the file cabinet list that you use daily, go ahead and move it up to the desktop.

Setting up a filing system is a highly personal process. You alone know that the file labeled "Rover" means the dog and also includes information on your five cats because that's simply how you *think* of the animals in your life. Use any language you like to identify files, as long as *you* know what you're referring to.

Using Your ABCs

Arranging your files can be done strictly alphabetically or alphabetically within a category. To set up the files by categories, think "Financial." Make a plastic tab that fits one of your hanging folders marked "Financial." Behind that tab, file the Bank, Credit Cards, Investments, and Taxes folders.

THE BACKLOG AND WHAT TO DO WITH IT

Now you've got a filing system in place. You can now proceed to organize your "inventory," if you have one— all your old papers in stacks or grocery bags or boxes— and relieve yourself of many, many pounds of paper.

QUICK ●━● PAINLESS

Use binders to consolidate like information. For example, gather rosters you've collected and put them into binders for easy retrieval. They can include your child's class list, the Little League team roster, and your book club group. If you save magazine clippings of house or garden ideas, put them into their own binder. Keep these binders on a shelf within easy reach of your desk.

Sorting Stage I

Start sorting. You might sit on the floor and pretend you're dealing a deck of cards. Your biggest contribution will (should) undoubtedly be to the garbage can. The rest of it should go into piles of like items. Keep in mind that, in general, you need to save only tax-related items. Those may include

- Medical bills paid
- All house improvement receipts
- Any receipt you've listed as a tax deduction
- All bank statements, canceled checks, and check-book registers
- All 1099s, W4s, and other tax forms
- All tax returns
- All correspondence from the Internal Revenue Service
- All year-end investment information
- Old calendars or date books

Sorting: The Sequel

After these papers are sorted, re-sort into years. You don't need to put things into any particular order—just get things into stacks by year. These stacks would serve as the backup documentation should you ever (heaven forbid!) be audited, so they should be paired up with that year's tax return. Then put all this paper into large envelopes or sturdy boxes. Be sure and label clearly,

IF YOU'RE SO INCLINED

Put copies of your important papers (originals should be stored in a safety deposit box at the bank) in plastic sheet protectors in a binder. Include passports and copies of birth certificates, baptismal, christening and confirmation records, marriage and divorce decrees, social security cards, and a copy of your will.

If you really want to purge, go through your boxes of canceled checks and throw out any that you don't need for tax purposes. Can you think of any reason in the world that you would need a canceled check used to buy dog food? You will happily end up with about a third of your canceled checks. They should be stored with the appropriate year's tax return.

being specific about the envelopes' or boxes' contents. They can all go on a high shelf in a basement or garage.

Ask your tax preparer how long to keep your tax returns and backup documentation. Most will say 7 years; many people keep them fewer years, but this depends on your comfort level.

Nonfinancial information is harder to purge. The test questions are "Will anyone ever need this information?" and "Does someone else have this information?" and "Could I get it from them?" If you can answer "No," "Yes," and "Yes," that's your ticket to start tossing merrily away with a clear conscience!

If you've found hundreds of your children's school and art projects, toss what you can part with and put the rest into boxes, one for each child. They will also go into long-term storage with old financial records.

At the end of each year, go through your file cabinet. This is when you pull out tax information and put it together for preparing your taxes. Because you've filed mostly tax-relevant paper, your file cabinet will be fairly empty after you've pulled your tax information. This is also a good time to toss the year's utility bills if you've filed them. Toss credit card statements and receipts if you don't need them for tax purposes. And you will start the new year with a nice, almost-empty file drawer.

MAKING QUICK WORK OF BILL PAYING

The following tips might help you speed the bill-paying chore: Put all bills as they arrive in a folder marked "Bills to Pay." If you pay your bills twice a month, put them into folders marked "Pay 1st" and "Pay 15th." The due dates of arriving invoices and how often you get paid will determine when you should pay bills. Write on the outside of each bill folder which bills get put into that folder.

Anything that requires a check to be paid later goes into the "Bills to Pay" folder:

- Coupon payment books
- The year's estimated tax payment forms if you are required to pay them.
- Charitable solicitations, but only those you have a serious intention of writing a check to. Then you can make the decision to make a donation when you're actually looking at your checkbook balance.
- Cards to begin a new subscription to a publication.

Using this system, you'll be able to find anything that requires a check because they will all, always, be in the same place!

Have in a drawer or basket all the supplies you need to make quick work of bill paying. You'll need envelopes, stamps, return address stamp (quicker than using address labels), and a calculator or an adding machine.

After you've paid your bills, review the lists above to determine which bills you need to keep and which can be tossed. It's easier to throw things away now than waiting until the end of the year to do it.

If you have a computer, get your checkbook and other financial matters computerized. The checkbook

YOU'LL THANK YOURSELF LATER

Pre-address envelopes to those people and businesses you often send mail. Include your return address, of course. Your computer will do this quickly for you if you let it!

management programs are wonderful and a great way to track expenses. *Quicken* by Intuit is terrific, and *Quick Books* is a more advanced version for small businesses. If you're unfamiliar with computers, take a class or get some tutoring to get you set up.

You can then graduate to electronic bill paying so that you rarely write or mail an actual check—it's all done by your computer's modem.

ANOTHER BINDER—ANOTHER WAY TO KEEP CONTROL

Rated as one of the most popular ideas I suggest in my seminars is putting together a binder in which to hold all your important papers. Let's christen it your "Important Papers" Binder. You'll find the materials for your binder, hopefully, in your file cabinet and safety deposit box, if you have one.

This is, if you will, a "living" version of the "End of Life" binder I suggested that you establish in Chapter 5. (Whatever you have in one binder, you needn't duplicate in the other. Just make sure that all your information is in one of them!)

Anything in this binder should be "backed up" one way or another. Ideally you will have originals in your safety deposit box and keep a copy of most items in the binder.

Here's what you put in your Important Papers Binder:

- Birth certificates
- Marriage license(s)

- Adoption papers
- Divorce decree(s)
- Passports
- Immigration or naturalization papers
- Any religious documentation, such as baptismal or confirmation records
- Social security cards
- Trust documents
- Powers of attorney
- Health care directive(s)
- Inventory of your safe-deposit box
- Military discharge papers
- Will

IF YOU'RE SO
INCLINED

Consider the option of having your important papers backed up by scanning them into your computer. You can create a backup disk of your binder, which is always good, and you will also allow yourself an easy way to update your binder when circumstances change. Just print and go!

Getting Time on Your Side

	The Old Way	The Lazy Way
Finding your 1995 tax return	A few hours over a period of 3 weeks	7 seconds
Looking up the telephone number of Girl Scout troop leader	35 minutes (Calling around to six different people to ask if they have it)	1 minute (Pulling out your binder of rosters)
Filing paid bills	Never happened	5 minutes
Opening the mail	15 minutes	5 minutes (because all the junk mail has been tossed, unopened)
Finding your symphony tickets	22 panicky minutes before the concert, making you late (they were stuck under the telephone)	1 minute, flipping through your "Pending" folder
Putting your hands on the lawn mower instruction booklet	Never did find that thing	45 seconds, in the Instructions and Warranties" folder

Quick Closet Control: Beating the Battle of the Bulge

Second to controlling the influx of paper, closets are the most-often cited disaster area in homes. Really, it's not you. Something mysterious happens in closets. Scarves and shoes, coats and clothes, jackets and racquets, umbrellas and underwear, boxes and boots breed in the night. If you're afraid to open your closet doors these days, you probably need to regain control. You know that to win any conflict, you've got to have a plan. Here it comes, and it's *The Lazy Way!*

THE ANCIENT BURIAL GROUND CALLED YOUR CLOTHES CLOSET

Let's start with clothes closets. Do you feel miserable opening the closet doors and surveying a mix of out-of-date, wrong-sized, impulsively bought mistakes, most of which need mending or ironing? Do you long to be a monk in a robe or a schoolgirl again, only because they gave you a uniform to wear? How many problems would that solve in your life?

Would you like to open those doors to find wonderful, wearable clothes hung in some semblance of order, everything visible, unwrinkled and accessible—just like in the magazines? Would you like to know what you own and what goes with what? Would you like to have everything you own fit you? Keep reading.

Divide and Conquer

Go through your closet with the following categories in mind. Toss or hang clothes, shoes, and accessories in separate areas for each category:

- Keep

- Clean, Repair, or Alterations (this will probably include the shoe shop)

- Consignment

- Thrift Shop

- Friends and Relatives

- Throw Out

- Undecided

If you're in doubt about anything, here are some closet rules:

This can be a tough job, so set aside a block of time without kids around or other interruptions. Play calming music, turn up the lights, arm yourself with a cup of energizing tea, set a timer for an hour, and go!

The Lazy Way

- If it doesn't fit, either get it altered or get it a new owner.

- If it's tired, shiny where it shouldn't be, yellowed, or stained—out it goes.

- Shoes should be in good repair—no worn-down heels or scraped leather. Put them in the Throw Out or Repair pile.

- Some things can be updated with a new hem length or a change of buttons. Put them in the Alterations pile.

- Usable things that you simply don't wear for one reason or another go to Consignment (if they're worthy) or the Thrift Shop pile so that someone else can benefit from them.

Each of these different categories needs a work session. You may want to work on one pile per session because attempting all of them at once is overwhelming—even to someone who thinks this kind of activity is fun!

Wanted: A Good Friend for a Tough Job

We'll work backward from this list of piles, starting with Undecided. This is definitely the hardest category, so you should allow 3 hours to get through it. (The remaining categories will be a cinch!)

You might enlist the help of a trusted friend for the Undecided pile because it's next to impossible to be objective about what looks good, what flatters you, and

IF YOU'RE SO INCLINED

If you've come up with a huge pile of usable clothes to be mended (to add to the huge pile you owned before you started organizing closets), get a head start and send the piles out to be done by someone else: the cleaners, your seamstress, or anyone you know who sews and would like to earn a little money. It will be so much easier to keep up rather than catch up!

what's in or out of style. (Here's where your friendship can really be tested!)

When a woman is charged with the job of organizing closets, she has the extra burden of the emotions contained therein. Every garment has a story, a life of its own.

Your friend's role is that of a good therapist: to empathize and listen to the story about your senior prom dress or the suit that you bought on your first trip to Paris, and then say in a clear, loud voice, "That was then and this is now. Get rid of it!" The story is not important in the context of purging and organizing. Keep the memories, toss the clothes.

You will be left with usable clothes, or those sitting in the other piles. You should also have, at this point, much more closet space and be able to see the floor and walls again. Thank your friend and offer to do the same thing for her someday. This was hard work!

Now move on to the next categories, which you can handle solo.

The Recycling Pile

The next pile is Friends and Relatives, who might happily use things you no longer use. Won't you feel better to have your clothes worn and enjoyed, instead of having them hang, unused and neglected, getting out of date, in your closet? Your fashion design student niece may love the fluffy beaded angora cardigan that you haven't been able to wear in decades. That woolly coat, now that

A COMPLETE WASTE OF TIME

The 3 Most Terrible Reasons to Keep Clothes:

1. It's going to fit when you lose those 10 pounds.

2. You're sure it will come back in style.

3. Your Aunt Tina gave it to you, and even though you never wear it, you can't get rid of it.

you live in Florida, might find a happy home with Uncle George in Vermont.

The lesson plan for this session is to get in the car, if necessary, and do the actual delivering of these clothes. Or go get boxes, label them, get them to the post office or shipping center, and wave goodbye to them.

Good Works & Tax Deductible

The Thrift Shop pile is a slam-dunk. Get used to making your favorite charity's thrift shop a frequent destination. Make it your personal mission to see that it is well stocked with your belongings several times a year! And don't forget to get a receipt (to put in your current tax folder in your file cabinet). Those little things add up.

Getting a Return on Your Investment

If you own good-quality, almost-new clothes, you might feel better about getting rid of them if you make a few bucks in the bargain! So check out the consignment shops in your area for your designated Consignment pile. Be sure to ask them for their terms and conditions. Consigned goods generally need to be clean, pressed, whole, up to date, and on hangers. (You might decide to sell these clothes at a garage sale. In that case, get them into the garage for the time being.)

The Final Touch

The last pile is the Clean, Repair, or Alterations group. Don't think for a second that people don't notice missing buttons or dragging hemlines, holes in seams, or plain ol'

YOU'LL THANK YOURSELF LATER

A small investment with a dressmaker to alter your still-good garments can pay big dividends. A nip here, a tuck there, sleeves slightly lengthened or shortened—all these modifications can make a tremendous difference in how something looks on you.
Ask a seamstress or tailor you trust for her opinion.

dirt. Handbags might need stitching, and shoes may need new heels. Get it all handled.

Don't be tempted to save all your old T-shirts, sweats, jeans, and pants for your dirty jobs. You need only two "outfits" for painting or yard work or washing the car. Toss the rest.

Now you will find yourself with a clear picture of what you own and what you don't own. It may be easier to put together outfits now because your wardrobe is suddenly visible. Mixing and matching will be easier. You should look better because your clothes are not wrinkled from being crammed into tight spaces on misshapen hangers. You should have more time because you won't spend as much time pressing and you'll certainly, I suspect, pull yourself together more quickly in the mornings.

A WORKABLE WOMAN'S WARDROBE

For life to work *The Lazy Way*, you need a good, well-coordinated system to put your clothes to work for you.

What's Your Closet Trying to Tell You?

Scan what's left in your closet after the Great Purge. Do you see mostly black? Navy? Beiges and naturals? Pastels? Whichever you see the most of is a good indication of what works for you. You can build on that color as a place to start.

Build on Three

A good way to begin building a highly functional wardrobe is by investing in three important pieces:

matching jacket, pants and skirt. The operative word here is "invest." Get the highest quality you can afford; they will last a long time, keep their shape and keep you looking good. Pick black, navy, or taupe—or whatever you consider your base color. These can be in any fabric, as long as it's good quality. Lightweight wool crepe, a silk blend, or microfiber twill are all good versatile choices and work for most seasons and occasions. If you experience extreme climates, you may need a summer set in a linen/synthetic blend, perhaps, and a winter set in wool.

Choose your three basics with your lifestyle and body type in mind. (Be sure and get help if you're unsure about what looks good on you.)

- Your jacket can be a classic blazer, fitted or boxy. It can be a short, fitted Chanel-type jacket or a long, straight one with no buttons. It can have lapels, a shawl collar, or no collar. Single breasted or double breasted or no fasteners at all. Fully lined, please.

- The pants can be classic trousers with pleats, cuffed or not cuffed, or slim and flat fronted. For most durability, they should be lined. For comfort, you may prefer a little elastic somewhere on the waistband. Your favorites may not have a waistband.

- Your skirt can be softly gathered and mid-calf length, or short and slim, or long and straight.

Your three pieces can be dressed up—you'll have a dressy outfit if you wear two pieces together with a silk

IF YOU'RE SO
INCLINED

If you're not sure, don't guess! There are plenty of people just waiting to assist you with your selection—so think of those sales assistants as your personal buyer of the moment and make sure you outfit yourself in a flattering way!

Do you forget the step called "alterations" when you buy clothes? Many of the things you buy need sleeves shortened, hems raised or lengthened, a nip in at the waist, or to be let out a smidgen at the hips. Don't overlook the importance of a half-inch—it really can make all the difference in how your clothes fit and how you look!

shirt or glittery camisole—or dressed down (the jacket over jeans or the skirt with a denim jacket).

However you mix and match, you'll return to these three pieces again and again. You can add fun stuff, or trendy, one-season fillers for variety, but these three pieces will be your ground zero for all of your wardrobe needs.

More Essentials

Everyone also needs, in some form, the pieces I've listed below. These work with the three building blocks listed above. You can adjust for your body type, climate and lifestyle, but choose quality.

- The forever classic and classy white cotton shirt looks great on just about everyone. Crisp and clean, it goes under a blazer or cardigan and over jeans or skirts. It can be thrown over shorts for the beach, or tucked into a wool suit for business.

- Ditto the classic silk blouse. (In off-white if you can't wear white.)

- To my way of thinking, a lightweight chambray (or pale denim) shirt is essential.

- A couple of pairs of good quality shoes and belts.

- Boots, either knee high or lace-up ankle ones, update a look quickly and keep your tootsies warm!

- The "little black (or gray, or red, or navy) dress" to take you anywhere.

Updating Three Wardrobes

Obviously, your lifestyle is going to determine what kinds and how many clothes you need. The stay-at-home mom, a banking executive, and a home-based entrepreneur each have different wardrobe requirements. Let's look in each of these three women's closets and how I'd suggest organizing them.

Tina the Mom

Tina is in the business of running a household with kids, dogs, and the car pool. She works at her children's school and casually entertains other families with children often. She, like most of us, has zero time to devote to her wardrobe and needs things that are easy to care for. Let's say she looks great in navy and that her beautiful olive complexion and dark hair are wonderful with bright colors.

Tina just emptied her closet of most of the old sweatshirts, sweatpants, tired jeans, and t-shirts. What she has left are a nice pair of chinos, some taupe corduroy pants she wears in the winter, one pair of jeans, and assorted tops. She's got one very dressy outfit that she loves and wears on special occasions.

Sounds to me as though Tina needs something to fill the gap between every day and chiffon. Here's what I'd put on her shopping list:

- A good blazer or jacket—probably in navy—would go over all her pants and jeans and dress them up to go to school or to a meeting.

Congratulations! You've pared down your closet to just the stuff you actually wear and you're ready to acquire a few well-selected classic pieces! Take a break and go see a movie, maybe you'll get some wardrobe inspiration from the costumes!

The Lazy Way

■ A pretty sweater or sweater set would serve the same purpose. This might be in red, which would go with her khaki-colored chinos, denim, and the corduroys.

■ A soft skirt, maybe mid-calf length in a small or bold navy and white print, would add another degree of dressiness to her wardrobe. Depending upon weight and fabric, she could wear her blazer or her sweater set over the skirt to change its look.

■ A soft, classic, tailored silk shirt in white would also dress up her pants and skirt.

■ If Tina is less conservative, she might love the look of a black leather jacket with her separates, worn with chunky black leather boots.

I'd be sure Tina had a couple of great belts to complement her chinos, jeans and skirt, a couple pairs of great looking shoes for when she's not in tennies, and a strand of pearls—just because!

Barbara the Executive

Barbara also has no time, and what she's got left in her closet is a short straight wool skirt in black, black turtlenecks, black pants and some blouses. She loves neutrals—taupe, cream, and natural tones. She's got to look professional every day and keeps long hours.

Barbara needs to "lighten up" all the black in her closet. Here are some ways she could expand her wardrobe choices and add some life to her look:

- A couple of jackets that mix black with neutral tones would give her a lot of variety. One jacket could be short and fitted, of black and taupe silk tweed. The other jacket could be long and slim in a neutral plaid with a bit of black in it. Both of these will go over her black skirt and pants but are different enough in shape and texture to create completely different impressions.

- Barbara can wear pants to the office, so she should add a tweedy pair of tailored trousers in a dark neutral to wear with her black turtlenecks and soft blouses.

- She loves turtlenecks, so she should get a silk knit one in a cream color to go with her new jackets and tweed pants.

- If she has the budget and room for them, I'd add a black jacket to go over everything, natural colored linen pants for summer and a long black skirt for variety and warmth.

Barbara's finishing pieces would be black boots, a pair of beautiful black pumps, and a very dressy jacket to wear over her black pants and skirts.

Kathy the Entrepreneur

Kathy has the best of both worlds: she can sit in her home office at noon in her sweats dealing with her clients and doing her own administrative tasks. Once a week she commutes into the city for meetings. She also

YOU'LL THANK YOURSELF LATER

You don't need to have a zillion pairs of shoes to be well outfitted, but you should be picky. As we've said before, buy the best you can afford—they'll last longer and look much better!

QUICK PAINLESS

needs to travel at times, often on short notice. She mostly needs clothes for her city visits and traveling.

Kathy is a dark blond and can wear vibrant or muted autumn colors. Her cleaned out closet contains jeans and sweats for every day, a muted olive green skirt, a pair of good brown pants and some tops.

I hope Kathy doesn't have to take a trip soon: she needs to go shopping! Here's where she might fill in the gaps:

- Kathy needs to start with the three basic pieces I described above. Let's say she finds a blazer, a long slim skirt, and classic trousers made of a fine, wrinkle-resistant microfiber twill. She picked a muted amber color that looks wonderful on her.

- A cream silk blouse and a cream sweater shell in cotton will give her two looks.

- A black knit turtleneck (or tank) and long matching cardigan will go over her amber pieces, as well as her olive green skirt.

- Both her brown pants and olive skirt can be paired with a jacket in a tweed fabric incorporating both colors.

- A couple of mahogany brown knit pieces in a matte jersey would be a boon while traveling. Slim, pull-on pants and jacket would work with shells and t-shirts and have Kathy arriving at her destination wrinkle-free and comfortable.

I'd urge Kathy to purchase comfortable shoes or boots in brown and light taupe. She could also use a couple of scarves with her colors mixed up in them. A long, dramatic microfiber raincoat in a light taupe or khaki color will coordinate with everything and travel well. She could dress up her at-home jeans look with a pretty cotton sweater set.

TRUE CONFESSIONS

Let's talk about your purse. Is it stuffed full? Can you find things in it? Is it heavy? How does it look? And just how would you feel if I asked you to open it up and let me inspect? Right now? If you cringe at the thought—because you haven't seen the bottom of your bag for a couple of years now—let's apply *Lazy Way* organizing principals to your closest companion!

- Give yourself a quiet 30 minutes to go through your purse.

- Upend it and let everything glide out onto a table-top.

- Guess what I'm going to suggest first? If you answered "Throw out the junk," you guessed right! Gum wrappers, empty stamp books, old envelopes, and grocery receipts can probably be tossed right away.

- Collect all the money that's been lurking at the bottom and put it into your wallet.

YOU'LL THANK YOURSELF LATER

Before you put something into the "I absolutely have to have this everyday" pile, think again, and be honest! If you only grab for that item once every week or so, it's not an essential item!

QUICK 🔘 *PAINLESS*

Think about color coding
the smaller bags within
your purse. Then all you'll
have to do is grab for the
right color, instead of—
inevitably—pulling out the
wrong one every time!

▢ Collect all the paper—the appointment slips, the charge card receipts, the school papers, an un-cashed check you've been looking for, and the letter from your brother—and cart them into your office.

▢ Gather the cosmetics in a pile. You may find your favorite lipstick among the brushes and pots and tubes. Throw out any dried up or old items and save the ones you must have with you in a pile we'll deal with later.

▢ Consolidate all your cards—credit, insurance, library, and video store varieties. Take the ones you don't use regularly into your office; save the rest in a pile by the cosmetics.

▢ Take out anything else in your purse that you don't need on a regular basis and put it elsewhere.

Interior (Purse) Design 101

Okay, now you've got a pile of stuff you absolutely have to have with you every day. (Do you ever wonder how men possibly get along with just two pockets?) Let's redecorate the inside of your purse.

Divide and Conquer

My system—one that has worked well for me for a sev-eral years—has been to break up my belongings and to put them into transparent, mesh, zipper bags. (Walker makes great ones, and I've seen others at the Gap, Target and art supply stores.) The transparent part is important so that you can see at a glance what you've got where.

Another option, though, is bags of different colors; you'll quickly learn that your credit cards are in the blue one and that your nail file is in the red one. I particularly like the varieties and colors of tough nylon ones made by Le Sportsac.

You can arrange your purse however you like, but if you adopt the idea of using smaller bags, you'll have a minimum of things rolling around on the bottom of your purse, and all like things—ideally—will be together.

I have two mesh bags in addition to my wallet. My wallet holds my checkbook, one credit card, my ATM card, and driver's license. My wallet is usually out when I receive a receipt, so I store receipts—flat and unfolded—there. If I need to make a quick dash into the grocery store, I can just grab my wallet and I've got everything I need to make a purchase with cash, check or debit card.

In mesh bag number one, I keep my other cards: video store, library, and health insurance, for example. I don't use them very often, but I do want them with me—just in case. I also keep some clients' keys in bag one. You may want your pocket calculator in your bag.

In mesh bag number two, I put my lipsticks, a small bottle of aspirin, a short nail file, breath mints and a tiny bottle of hand cream. You might add a small brush or comb.

Give a thought to those things that don't necessarily have to be in your purse and can be moved elsewhere. Here are some alternatives:

▪ Your umbrella might just stay in the car.

IF YOU'RE SO
INCLINED

Sure we'd love to be perfectly coordinated all the time, but not at the expense of getting things done. If you find yourself consistently saying, "oh no, it's in my other bag" then you should probably settle on one bag that can work for everything that's day to day.

- Maps, ditto.
- A small cosmetic case can sit in your car so you don't have to cart around touch-up equipment wherever you go.
- Be sure and buy travel sizes of everything you can for your purse.
- Magazines and files might be better off in a brief-case or totebag.

The Search for the Perfect Handbag

Another issue to consider is what kind of purse you use. Here's a checklist as you search for the perfect bag:

- How big? It should hold your things comfortably, but not be large enough to resemble a gym bag.
- How small? Maybe you'd prefer carrying a tiny bag that will fit into a larger tote or briefcase?
- How many pockets and zippers and compartments? You may not need the small mesh bag system if your purse has enough compartments to keep you organized.
- What shape? A long "feedbag" or hobo bag is going to send all your belongings hurtling downward to the bottom. Something shorter and wider is going to facilitate your finding things.
- What color? Here's where there are two schools of thought. I've convinced myself that I don't have time to change bags to match my outfits—except for

If you can find a purse you like that has a light-colored lining, grab it! (I don't know why purse manufacturers haven't wised up to this, but it can be terribly hard to see into the depths of a black purse, particularly in bad lighting.)

dressy events—so I generally carry a black purse. My friend, Patricia, shocked at this lapse, would never be caught dead in mismatched shoes and bag. It's really a matter of your preference, what your Mom taught you, and how much time you have to change purses.

What style? Here are some options you might consider, all with shoulder straps:

1. Le Sportsac makes a great line of washable, ripstop nylon bags in many sizes and with a wealth of compartments. They're practically weightless and are appropriate for casual and sporty situations.

2. Look at TravelSmith catalog's selections of leather and microfiber bags. Designed for the traveler, their bags would also work wonderfully for those of us who don't travel further than the grocery store.

3. A bag like Esprit's "Career Organizer" is a good choice for working women who need to carry a few files and magazines with them in addition to personal items. It's also large enough for a cell phone and a couple of mesh bags.

4. I've been meaning to try AmeriBag's "Healthy Back Bag," a sort of crescent-shaped leather or microfiber design that distributes the weight of your load by 30%—a lot better on your back and

QUICK PAINLESS

Your purse will never reach the depths of disaster if you make it a habit to edit it every night. Stand at your desk and take out the day's receipts and notes, and toss the debris. Really—it works!

shoulders than what we generally carry around. They have compartments to keep you organized and come in three sizes.

What To Do with Out-of-Season Clothes

If you're wearing seersucker, what do you do with your minks? If you can, move off-season clothes away from your regular closet space.

- "Borrow" space in the kids' closets. Just be sure they don't play dress-up with your gala clothes!

- Get portable racks for the basement or attic. Be sure to cover your clothes with a sheet.

- Try canvas-covered portable closets from organizing shops.

- Out-of-season shoes leave the closet (I put them into plastic bins meant for holding gift wrap and push them under the bed).

- Special-occasion clothing, like your tuxedos and Cinderella ballgowns, joins the out-of-season wardrobe elsewhere.

THE CLOSET INFRASTRUCTURE

Your first organizational task of the day is getting dressed. Whether you're getting ready to argue a case in court or walk the dog, you should be properly dressed for the task. And it shouldn't take you hours to get that way. If you've got your closet in order, you'll find it a lot easier to achieve that goal. Good luck!

Almost all closets can use a few space-expanding tricks, which might require hiring a handy person for a few hours and investing in storage boxes and organizing equipment. The money will be well worth it when you see how much more space you gain! Which organizing tricks you use depend on the size of your wardrobe, your budget, your closet configuration, and your degree of desperation.

Aiming High

One of the first rules is to get as much off the floor as possible. You won't believe how gratifying it is to vacuum the bottom of your closet, for the first time in years perhaps, once you've cleared everything off the floor.

Have I Mentioned Shelves?

I've seen very few closets that don't have room for an additional shelf above the existing shelf. There's usually lots of wasted space up there, and it's a great spot to store little-used or off-season belongings. Add a simple but sturdy shelf or two above the existing shelf over the closet rod. Think how doubling or tripling your shelf space will help your organizational efforts.

Getting Things Squared Away

Bins or boxes, sitting on shelves, can be used to hold what doesn't fit into drawers or can't be hung up:

- Scarves or pantyhose or baseball caps.
- Use one for gloves and mittens, one for ski clothes, and another for workout wear.

QUICK ☜☞ PAINLESS

Remember what dear ol' Mom said about hanging up your clothes as soon as you take them off? Well, she was right! The moisture and heat in them helps them regain their shape if they are properly hung up right after wearing. Important: Button a few buttons and zip up zippers after you hang them up, too. Fasten loose buttons and repair dragging hems before you put anything back into the closet.

Use shoe trees. They significantly increase the life and the looks of your shoes. You need only a pair or two; just get the pair out of yesterday's shoes and put them in today's shoes—while they're warm and damp—before putting them away. They'll air out in beautiful shape!

If you happen to have a collection of Spanish lace mantillas, by all means, put them into a container, too!

You can use cardboard boxes, but label them boldly so you can find anything you need on the most rushed mornings. The best container, though, is a see-through one.

Shoe Secrets

Shoes, even if you have enough pairs to qualify as Imelda's trainer, should be off the floor.

Buy a shoe organizer that fits in your closet. You can find them made in many materials in the organizing section of local department stores, as well as specific storage stores. They are generally hanging ones or rectangular boxes, divided into shoe-size sections.

You can often fit two shoes into one cubby to save even more space.

You might want to hang short things above the shoe organizer.

If you're out of closet space, but have sturdy doors, try a shoe organizer that hangs inside the door.

If you're out of floor space, put shoes into clear plastic boxes and stack them on shelves.

Don't Spare the Rod

Try adding a closet rod below your existing rod (at least partway across) and increase your hanging room for shorter garments like shirts and blouses. You can find kits to do this at storage stores.

- You might find you have to raise the top rod to accommodate a second rod.

- If your closets have incredibly high ceilings, you can put another rod near the top of the ceiling to hold a whole other wardrobe.

Hangin' High

How you hang your clothes affects how they look and how long they last.

- Invest in good plastic hangers. Using all the same style and shape enhances the tidiness of your closet.

- Double up by using suit hangers (jacket on top and skirt or pants clipped below) whenever possible to save space and to group an outfit together so you don't spend time searching for matching pieces.

- If you have enough full-length closet space, hang pants from clip-on hangers, either from the waist or the cuffs, whichever you find easier. This helps shake out wrinkles.

- Pants can also be folded over a plastic tube hanger and take up only half the hanging length. I do both: I fold my jeans and other casual pants over tube hangers and hang the good ones lengthwise.

Fine-Tuned Storage Ideas

Here are more suggestions for additional storage:

IF YOU'RE SO
INCLINED

Think about finding space in each bedroom to store the appropriate sheets, and you'll find that changing the sheets is a breezy task!

- The addition of sturdy hooks inside, along the sides or even backs of closets, gives you good hanging room for handbags, belts, and your everyday sweats.

- A board with three to five pegs can hold a lot of hanging items.

- Don't forget a tie rack for ties, belts, or hanging jewelry.

- You can set up a pegboard arrangement with hooks to hold scarves, necklaces, bracelets, and other hanging items. If it is arranged nicely enough, it could count as decorating!

- A expandable mug rack with hooks can hold scarves and other hanging accessories.

- Hats can be placed in pretty hat boxes on top storage shelves or simply tacked to the wall (push pins are good for this) as a decorative touch.

VARIATIONS ON A THEME

Linen and hall storage closets can quickly build up to overflow capacity. Here are some ways to keep them pared down:

- Purge the closets' contents first. Toss those ratty towels and shredded sheets. Give away duplicate items. Which coats and jackets have been sitting in the hall closet without being worn for years?

- Most of these closets can use another shelf or two. Determine if yours can accommodate more.

Then do whatever's necessary to make the closet work for you.

Good job. You've purged, you've merged, you've given away, you've thrown away. With all your worn sheets gone, you might discover that you need sheets. Treat yourself to a pretty new set. Perhaps all your white shirts failed the closet audit. Go out and get yourself a gorgeous one!

The Lazy Way

Linen Closet Lessons

■ Label your sheets so you know which size is which. Use a permanent laundry pen and mark the sheet's size on its hem (rather than the teeny label, which can take half an hour to find!).

■ Then label the shelves with sheet sizes to take the guesswork out of putting laundry away.

■ Put master bedroom sheets on one shelf and twin bed sheets on another to simplify things on bed-changing day.

■ If the linen closet is crowded, see if you can't find space in each bedroom to store that room's sheets.

■ So that bulky comforters don't take up so much room, I store mine by folding them in half and then rolling them up firmly, as you would a sleeping bag. A bungee cord holds them tight. Store them for the summer in an open plastic bag (so they can breathe).

■ Plastic boxes or wicker baskets can hold soaps and toiletries together.

■ Cleaning supplies can be contained in baskets.

The Coat Closet

■ If there's room, hang heavy-duty hooks wherever you can squeeze them in for backpacks, scarves, umbrellas, and bags.

■ Mittens and gloves can go into bins or into a vinyl shoebag hung on the back of the door.

IF YOU'RE SO INCLINED

Give everyone in the house their own bin for mittens, scarves, and hats—it will make getting ready to leave the house in the morning much easier, and you'll probably never have to hear, "Mom, where are my gloves?" again!

■ Place boots and shoes on low racks.

■ Don't forget to install racks and hooks at a height where children can use them easily.

Getting Time on Your Side

	The Old Way	The Lazy Way
Finding your purple and orange 5-inch-wide tie	15 minutes	You won't find it—you threw it away
Getting dressed in the morning	25 minutes (and it's a hassle)	10 minutes (and it's fun)
Assembling two kids' (not even yours) raincoats, rain boots, and umbrellas before school	35 minutes, and a lot of tears (mostly yours)	8 minutes with no tears
Locating the scarf that goes with your coral outfit	You gave up after 9 minutes because you were late for work	30 seconds: All your scarves are in the plastic bin with the green top
Finding a clean set of sheets	20 minutes, and who cares if they don't match? (same size, same pattern)	17 seconds, on the second shelf marked "Buster's bed"
Number of skirts needing hemming	Four that you can locate	One, the skirt you bought last week
Number of shirts missing buttons	Too many to count and in too many places to look	No missing buttons at the moment

No More Nightmares

How do you feel about your bedroom? Is it your sanctuary, clutter free and attractive? Or is it the stuff of nightmares? If you'd rather enter your bedroom in the dark and keep the lights off so you don't have to see the mess, here are some simple ideas for you to transform a disaster area into a peaceful retreat.

A radical organizing tip will echo what your mom always nagged you about: Hang up your clothes! This alone might make a major dent in the disarray in your bedroom. If your clothes don't fit in your closets or drawers, quickly go back to Chapter 8, "Quick Closet Control: Beating the Battle of the Bulge," and read about getting those closets into shape!

STARTING WITH THE BED: OUR REWARD AT THE END OF THE DAY

The bed. You do make your bed everyday, don't you? Doing this chore daily, along with putting your clothes away, will make you feel positively in control of your life, and can make a big difference in the way your bedroom looks—guaranteed!

If you've got 14 pillows or a collection of teddy bears adorning your bed, think about paring down. Some people don't mind spending half an hour each evening removing them so they can crawl into bed and another half hour every morning lining them up. They can be decorative, but I say you have better things to do with your time. Put them on a shelf if you must keep them.

Where It Goes

The bed tends to be the focus of the whole room. Be sure it's comfortable, firm enough, and big enough. Be creative in its placement. Have you thought about placing it diagonally, with a table built in the corner behind it? This way, you don't waste the corner space because it holds all your essentials, and it's a dramatic decorating touch.

If you use a regular bedspread over blankets and remove it from the bed every night, try hanging it on a quilt rack made to hold blankets. It keeps the spread off the floor so you don't walk on it and keeps your room looking tidy.

The Bed as a Storage Solution

Besides sleeping, look at your bed as a potential storage solution. Often overlooked, the space under your bed can hide more than just dust bunnies.

- A platform bed, with drawers underneath, is a real two-for-one piece of furniture.
- High bed frames are more than romantic—they've got room underneath.
- A bedskirt or bedspread that meets the floor covers up the whole package!

QUICK ⊙ *PAINLESS*

Obviously, a bed not squished up against a wall is always be easier to make. Try to place it in the center of the room, or at least with an aisle big enough to accommodate you between the wall and the bed.

What Goes Under There?

A myriad of things can go under the bed. They just need to fit into containers flat enough to slide under the frame comfortably. Consider storing things you don't need often, such as

- Out-of-season shoes
- Out-of-season clothes
- Skis and ski boots
- Tennis racquets
- Important papers
- Photographs or paintings
- Luggage

I use a Rubbermaid plastic box, made to hold gift wrapping rolls, in which I keep all my off-season shoes. In the fall, sandals and other summer shoes go in there. My really dressy, very occasional, shoes are kept there permanently.

THE BEDROOM AS A LIBRARY

Is the bedroom a reading spot for you? Are stacks of books and magazines high enough to conceal small burrowing animals? Here are some suggestions to store and hold your reading materials and minimize clutter.

Bedside Tables: How to Improve a Necessity

I've found that most bedside tables are so puny that a magazine hardly fits on the top of one. Think big and get

YOU'LL THANK YOURSELF LATER

Try duvet covers and discover what Europeans have known for generations: The duvet cover envelopes a comforter or blanket and serves as both top sheet and stylish bedspread. A real time-saver! They can be a bit unwieldly when you change them, but afford you absolutely effort-less bed-making in between. Just shake it out, and you've made your bed *The Lazy Way!*

yourself more space. Give yourself as much tabletop room on both sides of the bed as possible.

- Use tables meant for the living room.

- Find used cabinets or tables at garage sales, or buy new ones.

- If you can find a bedside cabinet with shelves underneath, so much the better. Often, though, the inside of a cupboard is 20 inches high, and wastes a lot of space. Get a shelf installed in the cupboard at around 10 inches, and you double your storage space!

- Try a headboard with cubbies.

The Round Table Solution

Round tables are an elegant option for bedside table space. They generally look better on just one side of the bed. Another piece of furniture can go on the other side; they don't have to match.

- Get something sturdy, tabletop-high, as a base. The base can be a card table or any piece of furniture that has legs and is sturdy enough to hold what you place on top of it.

- Cover the base with a plywood round (up to 36 inches if you have the room), purchased from a home and garden center or building supply store and cut to your specifications.

- Drape the round first with an old blanket or mattress pad (to soften the edges of the plywood). It can be just long enough to cover the round; it doesn't have to reach the floor.

- Cover the mattress pad with a beautiful tablecloth made for your new table (or use a pretty sheet that you don't even hem—just tuck it under at the floor).

- The bonus here is that you can hide stuff under this arrangement!

MORE BEDROOM CLUTTER-BUSTERS

Bedrooms, in some homes, can be the scene of a lot of family activities. Books, magazines and newspapers, toys, clothes and shoes, ironing boards, laundry baskets, hampers, exercise equipment, shopping bags, and a jumble of junk on the tops of bureaus and cupboards can all wreak havoc on one's sense of harmony. And a lot of clients have told me that a setting like I've described does absolutely nothing to encourage romance! So here are some ways to clear the clutter and make the bedroom a peaceful place again:

- Look hard for places to install hooks, a good way to get things up off the floor. A short wall, a space next to closet doors, in the closet, and behind doors are all spots you might be able to hang pajamas, bathrobes, your workout clothes, or your next day's outfit.

- Did you think you could ignore that exercise equipment heaped with clothes? Put away the clothes, and then start exercising or get rid of the equipment.

QUICK ⬤ PAINLESS

If your bedside tables don't accommodate all your magazines, books, and newsletters, use baskets for neat storage of the overflow. But use square or rectangular baskets, not oval or round ones: your walls are straight, as is the reading material. The rule is square things in straight-sided containers!

- Have room for shelves, an armoire, or cupboards? One piece of furniture could house all those things that don't fit anywhere else.

- A television set or stereo can be housed neatly in a shelving unit or cabinet.

- Think big: one large storage unit that holds books, a TV, and other belongings is more stable, and looks much more pulled together, than a hodgepodge of mismatched tables, cupboards, and shelves.

- If you end up with a lot of toys in your room, assign a basket to a corner where they can gather.

Don't forget: As with every other place in your home or office, hooks, shelves, and baskets are a brillant solution only if you *use* them! Every morning or right before bed, do a sweep and keep up with the assortment of things that have accumulated in the bedroom in the past 24 hours. It makes a tremendous difference.

Are you lucky enough to have enough space to create a little living area for yourself in your bedroom? A large comfortable armchair and matching ottoman for your weary feet, or a small loveseat with a cozy afghan, could become a welcome retreat from the rest of the house and provide a private place for conversation, reading, or TV viewing. Add a small table, perhaps, to hold a telephone or reading materials. A floor lamp can be placed behind the chair or sofa for good lighting. Make it pretty, make it comforable—just don't make these pieces of furniture collection areas for clothes!

IF YOU'RE SO INCLINED

Not a conventional solution, but think about using a wall-mounted telephone by the bed. It saves some tabletop space and keeps the phone handy at the same time.

LAUNDRY IN THE BEDROOM

Here are some suggestions to keep clothes clutter at a minimum in the bedroom. Since you often undress in that room, you want to funnel dirty laundry directly to a gathering point, before anything hits the floor or any other "resting area." Consider these ideas:

■ Have a place to throw dirty laundry so you don't have to leave the room to get rid of it.

■ Get a good-looking hamper and use it. Place in a closet or the nearby bathroom if you don't want to look at it.

■ Keep a mesh stocking bag (made especially to hold delicate laundry items in the washing machine) right by the hamper so that delicates can go directly into the bag as they accumulate.

■ If you have the room, try two or three hampers for the white, colored, and dark clothes, saving you that step in the laundry area.

BUREAUS, CHESTS, AND TABLES: CLUTTER MAGNETS TO CONQUER

Are the tops of your bureaus, chests, and tables covered with frames, scraps of paper, stray pieces of jewelry, empty coffee mugs, fallen-off buttons, old newspapers, coins, credit card receipts, pens, tea cups, pencils, and business cards? Here's how to set up a system to clear the decks:

YOU'LL THANK YOURSELF LATER

Basket hampers are often more attractive than plastic ones, but be sure they are smooth so they don't snag your clothes. Or find basket hampers with canvas liners to cover any rough spots.

- An attractive jar or basket for the coins. If you're a big coin collector, get a coin sorter.

- Just a couple of framed pictures, please; find another place for the rest or hang them on walls.

- Put the jewelry away, but avoid your underwear drawer: Thieves always look there first!

- Toss the newspapers.

- Books go on bookshelves.

- Move those papers you need to keep—take them to your desk.

- Find one place for the matchbooks. (And if you don't use them, don't bring them home!)

- Use shallow or stacking baskets to gather makeup and other miscellaneous items.

If you've got your office space in your bedroom, see Chapter 6, "Getting the Home Office Up to Speed," for pointers on keeping it neat and organized. If it's just a desk without a real purpose other than to catch clutter, think about moving it from the bedroom to a spot where it will work for you or another family member.

As always, vigilance is the key to keeping order. Regularly clear out reading material, clutter, clothes, and shoes. The lazy way to get organized is be organized, often and in small bites, and avoid exhausting marathon cleaning sessions.

IF YOU'RE SO
INCLINED

Lamps tend to add to clutter and can take up a lot of precious bedside tabletop space. Try wall-hung fixtures on either side of the bed. They can be ornate or plain, and usually have swing arms so you can direct your light for great reading.

SO, THE BEDROOM CHECKLIST READS LIKE THIS

Okay. Today's lesson is complete. Here's a checklist for you to follow for the the next 14 days. (They tell me it takes that long to get a new habit—and you want these habits!) Either do these things, or get the supplies you need to start making your bedroom an attractive, ordered, and harmonious environment that you really enjoy being in!

- Make your bed
- Hang up your clothes
- Put dirty laundry in hamper
- Big bedside tables
- Baskets
- Clear surfaces regularly
- Hide the kids

Enjoy your peaceful new surroundings, and sleep well!

Way to go! You can see most of the bedroom floor again, and the only clothes you can see are hanging on hooks. Treat your room to new curtains or that painting you've had your eye on.

The Lazy Way

Getting Time on Your Side

	The Old Way	The Lazy Way
Making the bed	7 minutes	7 seconds (using duvet cover instead of sheets, blankets, and bedspread)
Clearing clutter	Never happened	5 minutes (with baskets and designated places for stuff)
Collecting laundry	Search party	30 seconds (with hamper handy instead of scouring the whole room for things that might be dirty)
Finding the book you'recurrently reading	5 minutes	5 seconds
Locating the bedside telephone if it rings while you're asleep	They hung up before you could find the phone	3 seconds
Dusting off the top of the bureau	Took too long to even bother doing	1 minute

Calmly Cut Down on Kitchen Clutter

More often than not, the kitchen is the heart of family life. Not only do bodies collect there, but things—many of which are completely unrelated to kitchen activities—tend to accumulate in there, too. *The Lazy Way* to keep a kitchen organized is pare down (pardon the pun) the amount of stuff you own. (Have I mentioned purging? This is not an eating disorder.) You want to create a high-speed highway to help non-kitchen "stuff" make a fast exit.

Let me walk you through the purging process. Then I'll discuss some great gadgets and tools to expand your shelf and cabinet space. Finally, you'll find suggestions on how to put things back in order to keep order. Then, as your reward, I've listed some time-saving techniques for you to use in and around the kitchen.

FIRST THINGS FIRST

How about a mini-project to get your feet wet? Spend an hour under the kitchen sink (horror of horrors) going through the following steps that you'll use on the whole kitchen. This might require some haz-mat equipment or a large net. After you see how fast and easy it is to organize this space, you'll be motivated to tackle the rest. Here goes:

- Toss all the dried-up miracle cleaning products, the rusted steel wool pads, and the seven old toothbrushes saved to polish silver.

- Sponge off the floor of the cupboard.

- Line with a light shade or pattern of vinyl shelf paper.

- Hang a few hooks on the sides of the cupboard.

Now, start putting things—just the essentials, please—back into the cupboard:

- One powder cleanser

- One bleaching agent (such as Clorox Clean-Up)

- One dishwashing liquid

- One automatic dishwasher soap

- A trash bin that pulls out on tracks or attaches to the door, saving shelf space

- Dish, bottle, or vegetable scrubber brushes hung on hooks

That wasn't hard, was it? Isn't it a lot more pleasant under the sink? Now just do that again (and again) throughout the kitchen, and you'll have yourself an organized kitchen in no time.

QUICK ⬪ PAINLESS

Store items under your sink grouped in plastic bins, tubs, or a portable caddy. They can be pulled out easily, and if they tip, the mess they make is confined to the bin. Or, to make things even more accessible, place items on a turntable. If you've got small kids around, be sure to put childproof latches on this cupboard.

THE ZEN OF KITCHEN ORGANIZING

Purging is the key. The less you own, the less you have to find places for or put away. If you want an organized life, then extras, duplicates, and unused belongings gotta go. This is most true in the kitchen where space is limited and efficient work routines need to be established.

Time for Tough Love

Be tough on your stuff, and be tough on yourself. Remember, when you're removing things, every little bit helps—even that extra martini stirrer. The local thrift shop, friends, and relatives are usually delighted with your treasures.

Asking the Hard Questions

Kitchen drawers, cupboards, and countertops should undergo a quick inventory and merciless interrogation. You might want to use this list as a set of guidelines when faced with the question of "to toss or not to toss":

- How many knives do you really need to function?
- Are three sets of measuring cups two sets too many? (The answer is "yes.")
- Do you ever use the fast-food giveaway cups and trays?
- Ditto the mismatched patterns, chipped platters, and cracked dishes?
- How many times have you used that mixer/blender/chopper/shoe polisher combo appliance that takes up 15 cubic feet of space?

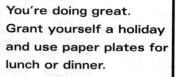

You're doing great. Grant yourself a holiday and use paper plates for lunch or dinner.

The Lazy Way

The number one cause for clutter is having more than one of the same thing—so take stock, and reduce your stuff to singles only. You might be surprised at how much space you find under all those "spare" supplies!

■ Couldn't someone else use eight of the ten loaf pans you collected the last time you were on a baking kick?

■ Just how many margarine tubs, yogurt containers, cottage cheese tubs, and coffee cans are necessary to sustain life?

Dumping Dishes

Dishes have special issues. "Theme wear" and special-event dishes should get extra scrutiny. Here are some questions to ask yourself when you open those cupboards:

■ The Easter punch bowl and 20 matching cups. Does it make any difference that the last time you celebrated Easter was in 1972?

■ The Halloween tea set with tea pot, creamer, sugar bowl, and ten jack o' lantern mugs. When was the last time you served tea at Halloween?

■ Those bridal shower dessert plates. Have you forgotten that you never give bridal showers?

Free the Fridge

Food—be it once-fresh, boxed, or canned—needs continual weeding out. You're not alone if you suspect that bags of flour replicate themselves in the night, or you're sure you never bought all those cans of cream of mushroom soup. And who opened three tubes of anchovy paste? Diligent deleting in the food department, as in the other areas of your life, is essential.

The refrigerator, of course, requires purging once a week, or at least often enough to keep the health department away. Don't forget the produce and meat drawers. They are great for hiding stuff, but things can get green and ugly in there when you're not looking. A good time to do this is "garbage night" so that tossed food doesn't sit around longer than overnight. This is also a good time to wipe up spills and keep up with splatters if you want to avoid big scrub-downs.

Another logical time to toss things from the refrigerator is as you're loading newly bought groceries into it. Don't push the new yogurts in front of the old ones; check the dates of the old ones and remove them or keep them in front so they get eaten first. If you know you'll never used those capers or are allergic to the three open jars of peanut butter, toss 'em.

Cupboards with canned and boxed food could use a scan at least twice a year. Check dates and donate still-fresh, nonperishable items to your local food bank. This is where you can unload some of the dozen cans of kidney beans.

Keep your eyes opened for announcements of food drives and use them as opportunities to rid your cupboards of unused designer salsas.

GO WITH THE FLOW

As you're redoing drawers and cupboards, rethink what goes where and if it might be arranged differently to ease traffic flow. Try to store things close to where they will be used:

YOU'LL THANK YOURSELF LATER

As you're putting the new groceries away, toss out the old ones, and you'll stay on top of refrigerator expansion!

- A triangular flow is best, so set up the kitchen with that shape in mind.

- The utensil drawer should be close to the table or the door to the dining area. That way, the person setting the table doesn't get in the way of the cook.

- The cook should have unobstructed access to the refrigerator and the stove.

- The refrigerator should be close to a clear counter area on which to rest things.

- Put dishes in a cupboard close to the dishwasher, if possible.

- Glasses should be near the sink or refrigerator; knives should be near the cutting board.

- Put least-used items up high, down low, or farthest back in cupboards, shelves, and drawers. Save easy-to-reach spaces for the most-used items.

- Group things that are used together when you store them. For example, put all your baking equipment and ingredients together in one cupboard. Gather supplies used to make lunches in one drawer.

REDECORATING THE CUPBOARDS

After you've cleared out and given thought to placement, give the cupboards a quick clean up. Then start refurnishing:

- Line shelves with a snappy vinyl shelf paper. This makes cleaning up spills and crumbs a breeze, and it looks good. Make it a light-colored paper; you want

A COMPLETE WASTE OF TIME

The 3 Worst Things You Can Do When it Comes to Organizing Your Kitchen Are:

1. Ignore your "standard operating procedure" when cooking.

2. Split sets: keep all your baking stuff in one place, and you won't have to run laps around your kitchen just to bake a cake!

3. Put an obstacle between the sink, stove, and fridge.

light and bright to increase visibility as much as possible.

- Try turntables (Rubbermaid makes good ones) to get everything within easy reach. If you've got adequate height in your cabinet, use two-tiered ones. This works especially well for spice jars.

- Spices can be stored in alphabetical order.

- I have two turntables with spices and herbs in no particular order, but one holds "sweet" spices used in baking (including vanilla, nutmeg, and cinnamon) and the other holds "savory" spices, such as rosemary, paprika, and pepper.

- Store envelopes and flavor packets upright in plastic boxes.

- Place your bottles of oil on a tray or a cookie sheet lined with aluminum foil. The inevitable drips then land on the tray, not the shelf. The tray can be taken out and washed occasionally, or the foil can be changed on the cookie sheet.

- Consolidate tea bags and other small items and put them in a tightly closed plastic container.

- Use plastic step shelves in cupboards, raising cans in the back higher for better visibility.

- Find wire racks that stand on a cupboard shelf to double your horizontal space.

- Allot yourself a small area in which to store a modest variety of your much-loved cottage cheese containers and margarine tubs. Toss—or recycle—the rest.

QUICK **PAINLESS**

Turn, turn, turn! Make it spin and triple the usable space in your cabinets with turntables!

Rack em'! Use that verti-cal space and try hanging your pots and pans—they'll be easier to reach, and save an amazing amount of cabinet space for other things!

The Pots 'n' Pans Puzzle

Wire racks are made to accommodate and make order of frying pans and pot lids. By stacking them vertically, you save cupboard floor space. You can also use wire racks designed to hold cookie sheets and trays upright and accessible.

Put pots and pans in wire or plastic drawers that pull out on tracks, so even the back ones become accessible. Turntables are also good for making the back of corner cabinets accessible.

Bulky pots and pans can be a real challenge to store. One of their characteristics, of course, is their round shape, and we're always trying to squish them into square spaces! However, some things can be done to minimize the amount of space they require. Search kitchen shops, catalogs, and large hardware stores for gear that offers some storage solutions for your kitchen.

If you've got wall space, try good-looking hooks (bolted securely, of course) on which to hang your most attractive—or most used—pots. Heavy wrought-iron pot racks can be attached to a wall or hung from the ceiling, making a decorating statement as well as getting your equipment out of cupboards and within reach.

Inside the cupboards, try large turntables to make all your pots accessible. They take a lot of room, but at least you won't be on your hands and knees trying to find the saucepan you need. Using the same principle, install wire racks on the floor of the cupboard that slide out like a drawer. All the back stuff is in your reach that way.

There are racks made to hold pot lids upright like books on a shelf and to hold frying pans horizontally in a stack like pancakes. They can save lots of room.

Cool Stuff

Don't forget that the tops and doors of cabinets, often unused, can be valuable storage spaces, but you're going to need some nifty gadgets to make the most of these spaces. Once again, you will find these things at your local hardware store, in catalogs, in large home centers, and in kitchen and organizing stores. They are worth the money if space is cramped.

- If you have a lot of stemware, install tracks (usually of wood or plastic) on the top of a cupboard. Slide bottoms of stems between the tracks, letting your glasses hang upside down, keeping them cleaner and, as a bonus, using that unused cupboard space.

- Screw cup hooks in the "ceiling" of a cabinet on which to hang coffee and tea cups.

- Wire racks or plastic organizers can be put on the inside of cupboard doors to hold boxes of foil and food wraps.

- Install a paper bag holder on the inside of a cabinet door to keep bags neat and out of sight.

- There's a wire rack made to hold lids to pots and pans that can go on the inside cabinet door.

YOU'LL THANK YOURSELF LATER

Install some hooks for your mugs and tracks for your stemware and kill two birds with one stone. By hanging them upside down they'll stay dust free, and you'll maximize the under-cabinet space at the same time!

Drawers: Divide and Conquer

Drawers can fill up quickly, so the trick is to limit what
you put in them and then contain those items. The
following tools will help and can quickly make order of
jumble.

Drawer divider units enable you to configure storage
niches to accommodate your drawers' contents. You can
find them as plastic interlocking boxes, plastic boxes with
dividers to adjust the length of compartments, or one-
piece plastic, wire, or rattan cutlery trays.

Plastic bags can be stuffed into cardboard cylinders
(such as a paper towel core or a 12-inch length of mailing tube). This method really compresses the bags and
saves space. Allot yourself two tubes. When the two
tubes are full, you know it's time to stop saving bags and
to start recycling them.

Everyone Needs a Junk Drawer

Every home needs one. The operative word here is *one*!
You can make it a bit tidier by at least throwing out
unrecognizable or broken bits and pieces and putting
the things away that are stored in other places. Just leave
the "junk" somewhat tidied in a cutlery tray. You're
allowed.

THINK CREATIVELY (OR LET ME THINK CREATIVELY FOR YOU)

Just because it's used in the kitchen doesn't mean it has
to be stored in the kitchen. What a concept.

Thinking Outside the Box

If your kitchen is near the garage, store your canned goods or paper towels on shelves in the garage close to the door between these two areas. Serving platters might go into a dining room buffet or credenza. Could linens move from kitchen drawers into a linen closet?

Furniture in the Kitchen?

Another option for more storage space is to buy a piece of furniture to hold things in or out of the kitchen: a small armoire in the breakfast nook or dining room, a vintage cupboard on a kitchen or pantry wall.

COMBATING COUNTER CLUTTER

Countertops can get really cluttered. Make a clean sweep and then organize those items you keep in view. Keep on the counter only those things you use daily.

- Consider replacing old, bulky appliances, like your avocado green electric can opener or your harvest gold toaster oven, with newer, slimmer versions, saving you counter space.
- Salt, pepper, and napkins can be moved to and from the table all at once in a tray or basket.
- Spatulas, wooden spoons, and so forth can go into a basket or crock by the stove.
- Jars of vitamins and supplements can live together in a basket or bin. Better yet, get them off the counter and into a cupboard.

IF YOU'RE SO
INCLINED

If you've got the room, consider an island—on wheels or not—for extra work and storage space. These are often topped with butcher block and have either open shelves or a closed cabinet underneath to hold bulky items.

QUICK • PAINLESS

Split sets of things. For example, even though you own a 12-place china service, not all of it has to be stored in the kitchen. If there are only two of you in the house, keep four sets handy and move the eight other sets to a less convenient area.

- Unless you use them often, remove cookbooks and canisters from countertops.

- Fasten wire racks made to hold mugs or placemats under the cupboards, over the counter.

- If things are gloomy in your kitchen, think about under-the-cabinet lighting fixtures.

HANG IT UP

If you're short on drawer space and closet space, think walls and what you can hang on them:

- Do you have space between your refrigerator and the wall it's next to? Install hooks for mops, the broom, and your apron.

- Hang small hooks by the stove for hotpads.

- A wire basket hung from a wall, under a cabinet or from the ceiling, can hold fruit and not take any counter space.

- A mug rack for cups and mugs keeps them handy and out of cabinets.

- Metal grids or pegboards with hooks can hold small gadgets and light, bulky items (such as a colander).

- Consider a decorative iron pot rack over the stove.

ALL THAT OTHER STUFF AND WHAT TO DO ABOUT IT

Most kitchens are the gathering spot for family and friends, Spot the dog, as well as papers from school, the office, and the mailbox, messages, rubber bands, shoes, sweaters, and softballs. Eternal vigilance is required to keep all these things moved out of the kitchen, and you'll undoubtedly need to enlist the family's help (that's putting it politely) to keep things cleared out.

- Paper's easy, now that you have an office space in which to deposit it. Try to get mail directly to the office, though, bypassing the kitchen altogether.

- Place a large basket right outside the kitchen. Into it, toss all the non-kitchen items that collect during the day. Your housemates should get used to retrieving their things from the basket.

- If you've got stairs in your home, place items you've found in the kitchen that need to go upstairs on the bottom of the stairs. (Of course, children will climb past them for weeks until they are sweetly reminded that they are to be taken up on the next ascent.)

Communications Central

Is your kitchen used as the family communications headquarters? Do messages get lost or do important communiques never reach their recipients? There are several ways to set things up so that everyone gets the information they need.

If a lot of messages are taken on the kitchen phone, be sure there's a message pad nearby—the kind that creates a duplicate directly underneath the original. That way, even if the top copy disappears, there's a copy of the message left for posterity.

IF YOU'RE SO
INCLINED

Purchase appliances that mount above the counter, under the cabinets or shelves. You can find can openers, microwaves, and coffeemakers designed to be used this way, as well as hand mixers, clocks, and radios.

Messages for different family members can be placed in plastic cubbies (one for each person), tacked to a bulletin board that has been divided (with yarn or a marker pen) into a section for each person, or on clothespins labeled with each person's name. You could also try tacking them to a wall by the telephone, using one small hanging clipboard for each person.

Vitally important messages for the whole family (such as "Mom isn't cooking tonight") might go on a blackboard, bulletin board, or glossy white board used with wipe-off colored markers.

You need to train family members to be considerate and thorough in message-taking and to consistently remove their own messages as they accumulate.

Keep in mind that magnets on refrigerators can be useful, but they create visual clutter. Keep them edited.

SOME TIMESAVING TECHNIQUES TO MAKE QUICK WORK OF KITCHEN DUTY

- When cooking, double recipes. Serve one batch and freeze the rest for another day. (Be sure to clearly label—with contents and date—anything that goes into the freezer.)

- Designate special drinking glasses in different colors for each child in the household. If they use them instead of grabbing a clean one every time they want a drink, you'll avoid the top-rack-full-of-dirty-glasses-over-an-empty-bottom-rack syndrome in the dishwasher.

- Make it easy for young helpers to put clean dishes away or unload groceries: Label shelves and cupboards with what belongs there.

- Find a safe place for knives. Try a wooden block with slots made for a collection of knives, or install a magnetic knife holder on a wall close to a work area.

- Use regular laundry clothespins (or what are called "French clothespins") to hold bags (such as potato chip, bread, or coffee bags) closed.

FOOD

If you're responsible for meal preparation at your house, make up one or two weeks of menus in advance. Most households subsist on, say, 10 to 20 regular menus. Write them down so that you don't draw a blank at 4:30pm when it occurs to you that dinner must be prepared.

You might keep a copy of this list in your wallet or day planner so you won't be caught in the grocery store without inspiration. It will serve as your shopping list, and you can shop for more than a week at a time with this list in hand.

Keep a pad handy where everyone can write down what food they just polished off or what they see is running low. It doesn't always work and it can require some training, but—in an ideal world—you'll always have a fairly complete grocery list going.

YOU'LL THANK YOURSELF LATER

If you tend to have a full freezer and lose track of what's in there, keep an index card on a magnet on the freezer door. Track what you put in the freezer and cross off what you take out. This system can help you avoid buying a sixth package of pork chops and forgetting that you're out of peas.

Shopping Strategies

Obvious, perhaps, but worth a reminder: Shop when no one else is shopping. If you're a morning person, this can be first thing in the morning before going to work. You'll need to run home to stash frozen foods, but you will spend so much less time at the store.

When I worked outside the home and had three boys to feed, I used one lunch hour a week to do my grocery shopping. You need to live near the grocery store to get perishables home or keep a large cooler in your car to hold cold foods until you can get home.

Lunch-hour shopping was a lot less crowded and went a lot faster than the worst time of all: right after work, an ugly scene you'd be wise to avoid. After dinner can be a great time to shop, however, and you're less inclined to impulse-buy on a full stomach.

RECIPES

If you're reading this book, you probably have too many recipes. Sit down some afternoon and throw out and sort them. Are you ever—really!—going to make that mango pomegranate filo-dough Napoleon? Doubtful! Get rid of cookbooks you don't use. Copy just those recipes you want and get rid of the book or stacks of Bon Appetits. Remember, it's the library's job to store books and magazines for you!

How you keep your recipes depends on how devoted a cook you are and how much time you want to spend organizing them. Make the jump from a bulging drawer to one (or two) of these options:

An efficient way to make grocery shopping a breeze is to make your grocery shopping list in the same order as the layout of your grocery store. You'll pick up items in order and won't have to backtrack.

ORGANIZE YOUR STUFF The Lazy Way

- Index cards. Use the 4 × 6-inch cards because you'll have more room to write. Store them in a box with tab dividers.

- Magnetic photo album. Recipes can be moved around or removed easily, and the plastic protective cover can be wiped off should Johnny take the hand mixer out of the cake batter while it's running at high speed.

- Scrap book. Paste recipes on paper with a glue stick.

- Three-ring binder. Glue recipes to three-hole punched paper. Use clear plastic sheet protectors for bulkier magazine or newspaper clippings, or just slide the recipes into the sheet protectors, skipping the gluing step.

- Join the 21st century and computerize your collection. There are software programs for this purpose, but you've got to be up to typing all those recipes! If you've got a scanner, your job is done.

If you've gotten this far, you deserve a treat. Now that you can find things in your freezer, locate the vanilla ice cream, and heat up some hot fudge sauce to pour over it. Enjoy!

The Lazy Way

Getting Time on Your Side

	The Old Way	**The Lazy Way**
Finding those pork chops	Days (possibly!)	1 minute
Putting together a grocery list	30 minutes	5 minutes
Locating the crock pot	Never found it; must have left it at Aunt Mary's	Never found it; gave it to Aunt Mary
Making a cup of coffee	7 minutes, after collecting coffee, spoon, grinder, coffeemaker, and filters	1 minute (all pieces together in a drawer under the coffeemaker)
Cleaning the refrigerator	35 minutes just taking out anything with a fuzzy surface on it	9 minutes, including a swipe with a sponge
Setting the table	13 minutes (mostly finding stuff and washing glasses)	3 minutes (You don't have to wash any dishes!)

Conquering the Chaotic Spots

Poor garage—often the dumping ground for entire families, and so rarely used for maximum efficiency. The garage project may take several sessions to organize completely. Be of good cheer when you attempt it, and be sure to wait for a warm, sunny day to help your mood. Enlist everyone's help for, say, 3 hours, and you'll be amazed at what can be accomplished. Most of these suggestions also work in attics and basements, so adapt them to your circumstances.

SIMPLY WHIPPING THINGS INTO SHAPE

As always, start with throwing away. Pull the garbage can into the center of the garage, and use it as often as possible during this process. (Did I mention that you should move your vehicle or vehicles out of there before doing this?) Then, what doesn't go into the garbage can should be stacked in those piles you love—you should be used to this technique by now—including thrift shop, yard sale, and give away.

You may be pleasantly surprised, if you've been tough about purging belongings, to find that you have more space than you imagined and that it is adequate for your needs.

You will probably have found by now—all in different places—13 extension cords, four cans of old paint, nuts and nails, seven bungee cords, parts to several flashlights, a few garden hoses, two Christmas tree stands, and a partridge in a pear tree. Group all those things in areas to determine what size container you'll need to store them in. You may need a quick shopping trip to buy appropriate containers. Then put like objects into plastic bins and boxes, cardboard boxes, bags, and baskets. Label everything in big, bold letters.

Containing the Garage

Here's a list of how many containers you might need to do some garage merging.

- One for electrical, such as extension cords and plugs.
- One for all the light bulbs you've come across.
- One for batteries and the battery tester.
- Phones and phone cords.
- Christmas ornaments and other holiday decorations.
- Jars (preferably plastic) in which to sort different nails and screws.
- A toolbox or two.
- A container for painting supplies.
- One for tapes, glue, and adhesives.

- One for small gardening tools, gloves, and so forth.

- One for ropes, twine, and string.

- A box of items for your next garage sale.

Think multiples. Whatever you have several of is the key to consolidating them and corralling them into a container. And if those containers are see-through, so much the better! Then up they all go, off the floor, onto shelves or into cabinets.

Keeping Order with Enough Storage Space

It's fairly obvious, maybe, but if you have too much stuff for the room available to store it, you've got two choices: Get rid of some stuff or increase your storage space. Presumably, if you're following this book's suggestions, you have already purged mightily or have plans to do so according to the guidelines above. If you're still stuck with belongings stacked on the floor or falling off existing shelves, then you've got to come up with more storage space.

Getting More Space with Shelves

Shelves present the easiest solution because you can buy them ready-made or have them built inexpensively to fit your exact space, and they make a dramatic organizational impact because they free floor space. Getting things off the ground is the key to great organization. (Garages are also more likely to flood and can be prone to leaky liquids, so it's even more important that your belongings are safely out of the way.)

QUICK  PAINLESS

Don't forget to carefully determine the depth of your shelving. Your top shelves, properly reinforced, can be quite deep—maybe a whole 24 inches—to hold bulky items. Just plan so that you don't end up with sharp corners sticking out at head level.

IF YOU'RE SO
INCLINED

Another approach is to lay plywood sheets on the garage ceiling beams, creating a sort of loft arrangement. Big, bulky items that are not too heavy (such as luggage) can be stored on this mega-shelf.

Shelves also offer the most efficient use of your space because they can be installed in multiples. Therefore, a wall that is 36 inches wide with four shelves on it yields 12 whole feet of storage space.

- Start with installing shelves wherever you can spare the space. You might try the length of the garage. You can install lengths of pressboard on brackets, or hire a handyperson to do this job for you.

- Shelves can ideally cover the entire expanse of the wall, but also work placed above whatever is standing on the floor. For example, install a few shelves over the washer and dryer.

- Buy knock-down, easy-to-assemble metal shelf units and set them up along the periphery of the garage. They are lightweight and can be found in hardware stores and home improvement centers.

- Another idea is to find old kitchen or bathroom cabinets (is anyone in the neighborhood remodeling?), and install them on garage walls. Of course, you can use new ones for this purpose as well. They offer a clean, dust-free, and dry storage space.

- Long-term storage goes up on the highest shelves or the most out-of-the-way place. For example, use your top shelves for banker's boxes, those cardboard boxes used to hold important but rarely used documents. These are generally old tax returns and related materials, negatives to photographs, wills, business and family legal papers, and so forth.

Get Hooked on Hooks

There's nothing wrong with plain ol' nails hammered in the garage walls—just make sure to find the studs to hammer nails into—to hold hoses, electrical cords, and miscellaneous items that haven't been grouped with anything else, or are too large to fit in a container.

Pegboards are also handy for keeping tools within easy reach. A handyman can install one of these perforated boards that hold hooks on which to hang small utensils and tools. They are best, of course, placed close to your work area—above your workbench, for example.

You can also use special hooks from the hardware store to hang brooms, rakes, and shovels to get them off the floor. There are also other types of hooks made to hang larger objects: bikes, luggage, skis, and so on. Meant for heavy-duty use, they are sold in hardware stores and catalogs, and most often are rubber-coated to protect your belongings.

Here are some other suggestions to try in your garage:

- You might find that storing bulky objects, like diving gear, works best in large duffel bags, hung on a hook on the wall.

- Collect sports equipment in a basket in the garage. One plastic kitchen-sized garbage can can hold baseball bats and tennis racquets upright.

- There are racks designed to group all the sports equipment together. You'll often find them in catalogs.

YOU'LL THANK YOURSELF LATER

If you're a do-it-yourselfer, try putting your tools into a rolling workstation. Then it won't matter what the project is, you can roll everything you need right to the job!

- Try a rolling cart with shelves under it. It may be just the answer to getting the recycling where you want it. Carts are also useful near the garage workbench to keep equipment and tools within easy reach.

- Camping equipment should be stored together, but only after it's been washed, dried, repaired, or refilled. Remember that it's easier to do it now, rather than the busy night before the camping trip.

- Keep an old bureau in the garage for off-season clothes or clothes waiting to fit the next child. Use masking tape to mark the outside of the drawers with the contents.

- Parts cabinets—the kind with lots of tiny drawers—are great for storing small things. More tiny items can go into jars, after you nail the tops to the underside of a convenient shelf. Just screw and unscrew the jar to use it or put it away.

Make a basket just for gardening tools that can be plucked up and taken outside. Consolidate all the family's shoe-polishing equipment, and put it in a basket with a handle so it can be moved to wherever shoes are going to be polished. Are the cabinets in your kitchen full? Try storing your canned goods on garage shelves.

The elegant, clean-hands solution is to call in a closet company. They'll measure, assess your belongings, and install storage units to accommodate everything you need to store. (But of course you'll still have to do the purging!)

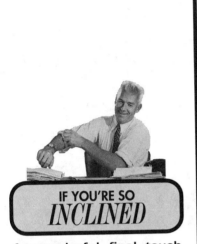

IF YOU'RE SO
INCLINED

A wonderful final touch to finishing the garage is a coat of paint. Think about how much time you spend in your garage—even if it's just driving in and backing out of it. There's nothing like paint to freshen and lighten up your surroundings. A good time to do it is after you've moved out what you're going to get rid of, after you've done any permanent fixtures (such as shelves), and before putting things back.

RECYCLING

You recycle, of course? Set up a recycling spot so that organizing these materials is easy to do and staging areas are accessible. The easier you make this chore, the more often it will happen. You may have an interim spot in the kitchen or hallway for recycling materials. Find an out-of-the-way spot nearest the garage door or under a table or countertop to place a bin with sections for the different types of recycling you collect.

Most often, everything then ends up in the garage. Get your kids to make the trek from kitchen to recycling center: Let them practice their aim tossing cans and plastic bottles into a bin. (You can even put a basketball hoop over the bin.) Leave space to accommodate bags and piles to be recycled so there is room to move around and make order.

Rules and guidelines differ in different communities, so you might need to adapt these ideas to conform to your city's norms. Your garbage company may also supply you with recycling containers. If not, be sure to get one for each type of recycling material if you're required to sort them.

Nothing multiplies faster than newspapers. Don't waste time struggling to tie up shifting piles of newspaper with string; just slip them flat into brown paper grocery shopping bags.

If your cardboard must be bundled, use #17 (big guys) rubber bands to hold the piles together—so much faster and easier than twine. Sometimes you'll need two

QUICK ⬤ PAINLESS

Keep a big box in the garage for used clothing destined for the thrift shop. That way, when you run across something in a closet or drawer that you know won't be used again, you'll have a place for it immediately. Keep the flow going from closet to garage, and you'll eliminate the need for closet-cleaning marathons.

rubber bands to do the job. I discovered these beauties at my accountant's office, where they were used to hold thick files together. Life hasn't been the same since. You can get this size rubber band at office supply stores.

HOW DOES YOUR LAUNDRY STACK UP?

Laundry can be a quick non-event in your life with the right clothes, equipment, and techniques. We all need to be clothed and to be clean on a more or less regular basis, especially the former, so we end up with yet another never-ending chore because we keep getting things dirty. Unless you're willing to wander around in your birthday suit or to send absolutely everything to the dry cleaners, you have to do laundry. Here are some ways to do it *The Lazy Way.*

This Is a Test

First of all, what kind of laundry situation do you have now? Be honest! Has it been a while since anyone had matching socks? Are most of the dresser drawers in the house empty? Are there clothes stacked or in piles in more than five rooms in the house? Can you tell the difference between clean clothes and dirty clothes? And is everything you own the same color from the washing technique you've used called "Grab a Load and Stuff It?"

Get a Head Start

How 'bout a head start? Go to the Laundromat and get everything washed at once. In two to three hours, you can accomplish what would take a day at home. Then recruit someone—anyone—to help you fold, sort, and put all these clean clothes and linens away. During this process, make stacks of clothes that need mending, those that need to be taken out of circulation, and those that need ironing. You'll know what to do with them as you get through this chapter. Now you can start from a position of strength—or at least from a position with clothes on.

One of the first steps to clean living is to straighten up your laundry area or room:

- Clear the area of clutter and old laundry products you haven't used in years.

- Put all the remaining cleaning products into a plastic bin for easy retrieval.

- Make space, if you can, for a flat surface on which to fold dry laundry. Use a counter top, bring in a table, or attach a pull-down tabletop to the wall.

- If you fold as soon as clothes come out of the dryer, you'll be almost finished before you even leave the laundry area. Scooping out all the clean clothes from the dryer, dumping them into a basket and then moving the basket to fold clothes uses a lot of energy (yours) and creates a lot of wrinkles that you'll have to iron out.

- Keep a basket handy to store clean clothes that you still want in circulation, but that are in need of repair. That way, you can pluck up this basket when

you find a moment to sit down to watch TV or chat with a friend. All your mending jobs will be in one place. Think about keeping your sewing box in the laundry room, too.

- Install a rack, hook, or clothesline to dry garments that should not be tumbled dry.

- Attach a fold-up bar to the wall to hold several hangers.

- Find a place to hang a short closet rod for damp laundry.

- Use plastic tubular hangers in the laundry room to avoid sharp creases on shoulders and the possibility of rust stains.

Down 'n' Dirty

Dirty clothes can be kept in hampers in bathrooms, bedrooms, closets, or a central hallway, if folks don't run into it. On laundry day, or when hampers are reaching the full mark, consolidate all the hampers in the laundry area. Here's where you'll sort darks, lights, and whites into three bins, baskets, or piles. (If any stack is taller than you are, you know you've waited too long for laundry day.)

Preparation Is the Key

A little laundry preparation will serve you well and pay big dividends in the long run. Your clothes will last longer if they haven't got stains on them, if colors haven't bled, and if they haven't shrunk beyond all recognition. Turn on the radio, take a little time, and do the following:

- Go through pockets and empty them.
- Turn dark garments inside out; otherwise, they fade quickly.
- Zip up zippers.
- Treat spots with pre-wash spray or stick.

Hand washing seems to have more or less gone out of date. You can probably machine-wash almost anything with the help of a washing machine's delicate cycle, cool water, and gentle cleaning products. Don't forget to use mesh bags for delicate items or those that might tangle in the washing process; pantyhose and bras are prime examples of candidates for a mesh bag.

Laundry Day *The Lazy Way*

Keeping clothes clean is not brain surgery, and there are ways to simplify this chore. First, gather the following supplies:

- One detergent, all-purpose, environmentally correct.
- One non-chlorine bleach, such as Clorox II or Biz.
- A liquid chlorine bleach, such as Clorox.
- One pre-wash spray for spots.

I use non-chlorine bleach for soaking light-colored clothes that can't touch Clorox, such as undies, nightgowns, and shirts. Put them all in the washing machine tub, let them gyrate around a couple of minutes to

QUICK 🔲 PAINLESS

Put all of your laundry supplies in a plastic bin, and you won't have to hunt for them when you need them!

IF YOU'RE SO
INCLINED

Have your water tested for hardness, and see if you really need to use fabric conditioner in your laundry. You may discover that you've just gained yourself both a little extra shelf space, as well as some cash!

dissolve everything, and let them soak for several hours. Then wash as normal.

Although we're advised to use non-chlorine bleach with colors, I find that some dark colors tend to fade rather rapidly using this technique. Use a pre-wash spray on spots and dark-colored garments, and avoid bleach. Be sure to turn dark clothes inside out before washing. See if these tricks don't help your laundry stay a little more colorful.

Chlorine bleach is great for all-cotton whites. If you have teenage boys who wear white socks, you'd probably give up your spouse before you gave up Clorox. It's also great for white linens and white clothes. Again, the soaking routine is valuable; time has a way of working out the grime while you do something else. Ironically, it may be easier to care for all white clothes—if they're 100% cotton and can be bleached—than it is to keep light colors clean.

You Decide

On the list of optional laundry products goes:

- Anti-static products: If you're dependent on them, be my guest, but I've never seen an overwhelming need for them. Do you really want another product to buy, another product to store, and another product to remember to use?

- Fabric conditioner: Unless you have extremely hard water, is it essential? Test a load or two without this product to see if you just inherited this habit from your mother.

■ Soap for washing delicate laundry: If you can't live without your Woolite, by all means keep it.

Wrinkle-Free

Pull warm permanent press items out of the dryer immediately and hang them up. You'll save yourself a lot of wrinkles this way.

Ironing can be stored on hangers, often on the hangers they dried on. Put flat items into a bin. It's not a pretty sight, but the most efficient way to get ironing done is to keep the ironing board and iron at the ready. If you've got a laundry room, you may enjoy this luxury.

Cleanly Distributed

The distribution system is important because this is where newly clean clothes can get mixed in with dirty stuff. There are two ways to handle it to avoid confusion.

Stack clean, folded laundry in piles by person or room, and stack them in reverse order of how you'll put them away. As you wander through the house, you can drop off one pile at a time.

If you've got the room, stack clean laundry on shelves labeled with each person's name. They can come and retrieve their own laundry and put it away.

Share the Wealth

Laundry can be a shared task and one you might get kids involved in at an early age. (This is assuming you're not one of those people who would never let anyone near their clothes or washing machine.) Both collecting dirty

YOU'LL THANK YOURSELF LATER

Set up your own "laundry pick up" station, and keep the clean and dirty separated. If you make a spot on your shelves for each person to collect their own clean laundry, you'll also be able to lighten your own workload a bit.

laundry and distributing clean laundry can be fairly easily delegated and will relieve the burden of the main laundry person in the household:

- Picking up all dirty laundry from rooms, collecting towels, bathmats, and sheets, and emptying hampers is one job.

- Putting away clean clothes is another.

- Try putting all clean laundry in a central spot (a large bed, for example) and let everyone claim his or her own clothes.

- Assign someone the job of folding dish towels, sheets, and bathroom linens.

Let's Make a Deal

Another issue to take up with family members is how much laundry is generated because of sloppiness. Do your adorable children grab a clean towel every time they shower because the last towel they used is still damp on the bathroom floor? Does everything automatically get shoved into the hamper whether or not it's really dirty? Do some things get washed and dried when all they need is a pressing? And do clean clothes get mixed in with dirty ones in bedrooms? At a family meeting, or individually, try to establish some systems and quotas for laundry.

The Teen Clean Scene

Can your teenagers do their own laundry? They might enjoy the autonomy, and it could be worth the time

A COMPLETE WASTE OF TIME

The 3 Worst Things You Can Do with Household Laundry Are:

1. Try and do everything yourself

2. Don't set up household laundry systems

3. Wait for the dog to do it for you

you'll need to spend training them. Have a checklist posted so that all the steps are taken to completion. They need to understand that the washer and dryer are not to be left with clothes in them when the next person needs to use the machines. Be sure to institute a schedule for each teen. Otherwise, you may find that emergency laundry sessions are regularly being conducted at midnight.

The Game Plan

When to do laundry? It really depends upon what works for you. Some people swear by doing a little every couple of days or as soon as they have a load of one type gathered (my method). Others save up and have marathon laundry sessions. Marathons work only if you've got enough underwear and clothes to last until the next session. Avoid at all costs the stressful children-without-clean-clothes scene in the early-morning panic hour. Remember that kids normally look at their clothes situation only as they're getting dressed—not the night before.

In any case, it helps to have a deadline set for yourself to do laundry so that a dirty clothes cycle can be considered "done" at least once a week. If everyone's deadline to deposit dirty laundry is Sunday evening, then perhaps by Tuesday you'll be crossing laundry off your to-do list. And hopefully you won't be thinking about it until the following Sunday evening.

A wonderful piece of equipment that actually "shrinks" your belongings is the "Space Bag Storage

YOU'LL THANK YOURSELF LATER

Think about laundry when you're buying clothes. Will they fit into your wash program, or will they require special handling? If you're like most of us, you want to avoid hand washing and dry cleaning as much as possible. Don't let the thrill of shopping blind you to the reality of maintenance once you get your garment home.

System" from Solutions catalog (as well as other places). You place puffy items such as sweaters or bedspreads into special plastic bags that have a nozzle on them. Attach your vacuum cleaner to the nozzle, pulling out all the air in the bag. Presto! You have the smallest possible "package" left to store. Then you simply stack your supply of plastic bags in drawers, closets or shelves. When you want your sweaters again come Fall, just break the seal of the bag and retrieve the goods. More good news: the bags can be reused!

Getting Time on Your Side

	The Old Way	The Lazy Way
Finding two matching navy blue socks	60 minutes	30 seconds
Locating a Phillips head screwdriver	40 minutes	5 minutes
Finding your boxes of holiday decorations	1 1/2 hours	50 seconds
Hours per week spent doing laundry	4	2
Hours per week spent ironing	3	1
Collecting every empty aluminum can in the house	28 minutes	2 minutes

twelve

Kids and Clean-Up: It Can Be Done!

Let's get one thing straight. Life isn't going to be totally organized with the addition of kids in your life. The sooner you resign yourself to the fact that they simply don't care about being organized, the less stress you will feel. I've seen more mothers drive themselves crazy (I'm in this group, mind you) because the LEGO®, blocks aren't all together and the puzzles are missing some pieces and there are sizes 3 to 10 in their daughter's closet because she grew faster than they could clean out her closet. But there are ways to maintain a semblance of order, encourage good habits in your children, and keep yourself sane.

Keep in mind that what you are trying to accomplish is not tormenting your children (or yourself), but helping them help themselves. Not only do kids need to know that their parents are not their servants, but they also need to gain both life skills and the self-esteem that comes with acquiring and mastering new responsibilities.

In this chapter, I'm going to present some ideas to get kids' rooms in order and suggestions for storing the multitude of toys, books, clothes, and other belongings they collect. Then I'll discuss the subject of children and chores (no, really!) and how to get them to participate in the business of life in a family.

BUYING IN

To start, parents need to set up systems, one at a time, enlisting their children's help in the process. For example, here are some tips to organize their rooms:

1. Ask them if they are satisfied with the current furniture arrangement or if they'd like it changed. Rearrange, if it seems reasonable, and you may get them more invested in how their room looks.

2. Go through clothes, books, and toys together. I've found that kids are usually very willing to donate their unused belongings to less fortunate kids. Fill bags with cast-offs and let them accompany you in delivering them to the church or thrift shop.

3. Do you have a source to resell books? Make a deal: They can choose new books with the proceeds from selling old ones.

4. Let them choose among different bins, buckets, and boxes and decide which toys should go into which containers and where they should be kept.

Don't forget to praise your kids for the slightest efforts to keep up their end of the bargain. Remember that this does not come naturally to them, and every small success should be acknowledged with verbal encouragement, a special treat for dessert, or perhaps a new book.

The Lazy Way

Make a Deal

How and when to tidy up is a matter of your personal tolerance of chaos and the kids' willingness (usually hovering around the 0 mark). If they are old enough to make pacts with you, make agreements on how often different chores will be done. Obviously, this is going to have a relatively low success rate, kids being the crafty devils they are, but an agreement will give you a baseline from which to negotiate.

Toy pick-up is a logical kid's job. Discuss the timing with them. Once a week is usually too seldom and might get overwhelming, every day is good, and after every play session is best. Like all systems, the more often you use it, the better it works. Go through the same routine about clean clothes and dirty ones. Will they put clean clothes away or will you? Decide together where dirty clothes go.

Together, go through a short list of what they can do to keep their rooms tidy, and when, and try to fan the "pride of ownership" spark in them. Perhaps a new "Bambi" bedspread would be an incentive to keeping order. They might love to see their dolls or car collection packed in cute totes with their names on them. A framed mirror or poster might feel like real "decorating" and inspire some pride. The promise of having a story read to them after the job has been done can be a real reward. And, of course, ice cream and money are usually effective motivators. Use any trick that works is my advice!

A COMPLETE WASTE OF TIME

The 3 Worst Ways to Organize a Child:

1. Scream and yell about cleaning up.

2. Set up too-elaborate systems that are beyond your child's ability to maintain.

3. Assume that she cares about neatness and order.

PINT-SIZED STORAGE IDEAS

You've seen it happen: from clean to chaos in 60 seconds. There is so much stuff, so much of it is tiny, and so much of it is vitally important to your kids. Children have special storage needs; what you do in *your* room often doesn't apply in the nursery or playroom. The following sections offer some storage ideas and ways to keep rooms low-maintenance.

Getting Hooked

Belongings might get up off the floor more often if there are plenty of hooks around, placed at kid height, in their rooms, closets, and bathrooms. (For some reason, kids have a hard time with hangers; you'll find hooks are much more child-friendly.) Here's where you want hooks and what you might want to hang on them:

- To hang up tomorrow's clothes.
- Backpack.
- Robe and pajamas.
- In the closet to hang your ballerina's tutu or King Kong's costume.
- On walls or in the closet for a queen's supply of jewelry.
- On the back of their bathroom door for a dirty laundry bag.

Small-Scale Organizing

Now, for the stuff you can't hang. It needs to get up off the floor, and similar bits and pieces need to be grouped

IF YOU'RE SO
INCLINED

Look for specialty hooks that match the theme of your child's room, such as Disney characters or their favorite comic book hero, and get their play-time involved in their clean-up time!

and put into containers. Put all the Halloween costumes and masks together in plastic boxes, gather all Scouting equipment into a container, and put gym wear or sports gear into duffel bags. That way, when it's time to play with cars, they're all together somewhere, and when it comes time to put things away, there is always a place for them.

Buy colorful containers and let kids decide which toys go into which. Everything from cottage cheese containers to shoeboxes are potential storage solutions.

YOU'LL THANK YOURSELF LATER

If you've got a toddler who plays by Mom or Dad in the kitchen or office, keep a drawer or bin in those rooms filled with a supply of toys.

- Puzzles can be put into plastic bags.
- Buckets, with or without lids, can be used for building toys, such as LEGO® blocks or Playmobil figures.
- If they're not on shelves, books can be consolidated in plastic boxes.
- Zip-locking plastic bags can be used for tiny stuff: beads, Barbie shoes, marbles, or rock collections.
- Egg cartons are also good for tiny stuff.
- Plastic (or recycled cardboard) shoeboxes are handy.
- Dishpans and refrigerator containers are good for organizing kids' stuff.
- Big mesh bags, meant for laundry, can be good for holding cumbersome toys.

Using Furniture to Your Advantage

Would bunk beds work in your child's room? They serve as a place for overnight guests, offer a home for stuffed animals, and make swell fortresses or tents. Trundle beds

Recycle the toy supply occasionally. In the dead of night, pull a third of the current inventory of toys and books and stash them out of sight. (This is where the high top shelf of their closet comes in handy.) On a rainy day or a bored day or a sick day, pull out the hidden supply. It will be like Christmas—at least for a few hours.

are the low-profile version of bunk beds; they provide an extra sleeping spot that can be pushed under the child's bed, taking up the space of only one bed. There are also beds with pull-out drawers built under them; these are great extra storage.

If you're handy or have a good carpenter, build your child's bed up high on a platform (sort of the top half of a bunk bed). The area underneath the platform can be used as more play room or a "work" area with a desk and shelves.

Be sure your children have adequate workspace for their homework. A simple desk, a good lamp, and near-by shelves will help them—if anything can—establish good study habits.

Other space-savers:

- Place a dirty laundry hamper or basket in their closets.

- Duvet covers work great for kids' beds; they can just be shaken into place and look somewhat tidy.

- Use wall-mounted light fixtures to replace table lamps, which can tip, break, or pose a fire hazard.

- Be sure there are large wastepaper baskets close at hand in children's bedrooms and bathrooms.

Maxing Out the Closet

Most kids' closets are often wasted space; they rarely need all the hanging room available to them. Here are some ways to use that valuable space:

- Move a bureau into the closet for clothes.

- Install shelves in at least half the width of the closet. Be sure to leave enough room so their largest toy containers can slide right under the lowest shelf.

- A bookcase can also serve you well in the closet. Just be sure it's anchored to the wall in case your active toddler starts climbing.

- Add a hanging rod below the existing one to double hanging space and put it within your child's reach.

- If their closet has the standard one-shelf-above-the-rod, you probably have room to install an additional shelf above it for out-of-season clothes or long-term storage.

- Don't forget hooks along any available sides or back of the closet.

- Built-in or standalone wire drawers are an alternative to a bureau; they're great for clothes.

- Stash toys, books, or folded clothing on shelves and close the closet doors on clutter!

- By stashing furniture in the closet, you'll gain more floor space for play.

EMERGENCY MEASURES, OR . . .

If systems have failed for awhile, and you're desperate to see the floor of their rooms or find the pet rat that has been missing for a week, here's a good way to make it happen fast: do a Quick Blitz. Spend 10 minutes—set a timer—with each child, and see how many things can be

Congratulations! You've added hooks, and the children use them. You've got all the books on shelves and TinkerToys™ in a plastic tub. You've seen the floor of the kids' rooms for a whole week now. Treat them and yourself to a burger dinner or a matinee. Remember the purpose of all this organizing is to make more time to enjoy your children!

The Lazy Way

put away on shelves and bins, thrown out, or dumped into the laundry hamper in that period of time. It's amazing how much you can accomplish! Kids really get into beating the clock and having you to compete against. It's not the deep-clean method or an approved system of organizing, but it's good in an emergency—and you might find the rat.

The school papers you keep can go into a large envelope labeled with your child's name and the year. At the end of the year you'll have, if not a scrap book, at least each child's creations consolidated and dated for posterity! Start a new envelope at the beginning of every school year.

. . . What Labor Laws?

You may have an upstairs maid and a downstairs maid as well as a nanny for each child. They still need the responsibility of chores and the good feeling that comes with fulfilling their obligations. It's so much easier to teach these concepts when they're little instead of suddenly telling teenagers that they've got to perform.

This takes training and patience, which is probably in short supply if you've got kids and work and are feeling overwhelmed. But if you can stop long enough to give them the tools—and take the time for training—to manage age-appropriate chores, the rewards will be tremendous, both for you and your children.

It's never too early to get kids working, and they really can make valuable contributions as tiny people. Besides, they like some sense of routine and order in their lives. Start with small, manageable tasks and work

QUICK ⬤ PAINLESS

Place a large laundry basket in a central location to collect school papers and works of art as backpacks are emptied every day. Or use a kitchen drawer to collect these treasures, or put a basket in the hall coat closet. Every once in awhile, with (or without) your child, go through and pull out the keepers. The rest can be tossed or distributed to grandmothers and other interested parties (in pre-addressed envelopes you have handy in the office).

up to bigger responsibilities. As a working single mother of three boys, I got very used to delegating. (Just ask them, and they'll tell you about their childhoods of hardship and agony!)

What works well is to make a chart and post it on the refrigerator door, listing jobs and who is to do them. Somehow, seeing it in print makes it a little more official and slightly less prone to "discussion." Get your kids involved in the creation of your family job chart. They can address the issues of who does what, whether to rotate jobs or keep the same ones, what days they are performed, and so forth. You'll want to end up with a realistic list of jobs, appropriate for each child and their ages, interests, and capabilities.

A partial job chart is shown below, listing a month's jobs by week.

A COMPLETE WASTE OF TIME

The 3 Worst Ways to Handle Chores Are:

1. Don't delegate them.

2. Don't post a chore list where everyone can see it.

3. Assign all the "icky" jobs to one kid.

Job Chart

Week of	Jan. 1	Jan. 7	Jan. 14	Jan. 21
Make Lunches	Niklas	Douglas	Thomas	Niklas
Collect Laundry	Douglas	Thomas	Douglas	Thomas
Take Out Garbage	Niklas	Douglas	Thomas	Niklas
Set Table	Thomas	Thomas	Thomas	Thomas
Clear Table	Niklas	Niklas	Niklas	Niklas
Empty Dishwasher	Douglas	Douglas	Douglas	Douglas

Get your kids involved at an early age with making breakfast and boxed lunches. They'll feel like "big kids," they'll have special time with you, and you'll get some extra help—what more could a busy parent ask for?

You might prefer to make a chart divided into columns labeled Monday through Sunday, or divide chores up by each child. Whatever works for you and your family is the system to use.

Two jobs I delegated to the boys were kitchen-related: making breakfast and packing lunch boxes. You can start amazingly early with these chores. Be sure to write down everything they need to know and walk them through the procedures as many times as necessary to make them feel competent.

I made a chart with five breakfasts listed, one for each day of the week. Then I did the same for lunch menus, listing all the parts required to assemble lunch boxes for 5 days. Here's how the breakfast chart looked:

Breakfasts

Monday	Tuesday	Wednesday	Thursday	Friday
Oatmeal	Cold Cereal	Frozen Waffles	Cream of Wheat	Fruit Smoothie
Juice	Orange	Juice	Banana	Juice
Toast	Toast	Yogurt	Toast	English Muffin

Anything that needed specific instructions was also on the chart, saving them frustration and endless questions to you about how to do things:

Oatmeal

1 cup oatmeal

2 cups water

Smoothie

Blend 1 banana and 5 strawberries in 3/4 cup orange juice.

Add 2 scoops nonfat frozen yogurt and blend again.

I can't guarantee that you'll be leisurely sipping coffee and reading the newspaper cover to cover every morning while the kids are handling things, but they will be involved and they will contribute to the day!

Kids' Organizing Jobs

Not every kid is going to go for this bait, but there are those who like little organizing projects:

- Supply them with coin wrappers and a coin sorter and let 'em make order of those jars of coins.

- Ask them to sort screws, nuts, bolts, and nails in plastic jars.

- See if they'd like to get the videos upright or books arranged by size.

- They might like to pair matching socks while you fold laundry.

- Hire an older kid to enter names and addresses in the computer for your address book.

Congratulations! You've gotten your kids to help with making a healthy breakfast! Plan a special weekend with your little helpers—you all deserve some fun!

The Lazy Way

KIDS' CLOTHES

From buying them, cleaning them, mending them, storing them or getting kids to wear them, the combination of clothes and kids can create some conflicts. Because they're outgrowing things so fast, keeping them clothed is an ongoing chore, but one that can be done without too much pain.

Socks, the Bane of Laundry Day

Staring at piles of clean laundry, the question of who belongs to what can be a perplexing puzzle. It certainly was for me when I had two boys almost, but not quite, the same size. I frequently guessed incorrectly which pair of socks belonged to which son. I figured out that how I shopped for their clothes simplified identification problems later on. Here are a couple of systems worth trying:

- Buy each child socks in a different color (at least until they insist on making these decisions for themselves) so that they—and you—always grab the right sock for the right kid. They may not match exactly in style, but they'll at least go out the door wearing two socks of the same color! This system makes sorting laundry much easier as well.

- You can use the same principle when buying underwear for kids. I bought one son solid-colored briefs, the second son patterned ones, and the third one always got white ones. Slick!

- Try labeling the toe section of each pair of socks (with a permanent marker or fabric pen); two matching socks are marked "1," two more matching socks (the second pair) are marked "2," and so on.

MAINTAIN, MAINTAIN

As with all systems, regular (and I do mean daily) maintenance ensures that you keep up. End play sessions a few minutes early so that there is time for clean up. Instead of shrieking about "cleaning up this disaster area," try to make a game of how fast they can get all the game pieces together in their box, or who can bring you the most books while you put them back on the shelf. (If they detect the panic in your voice, they'll know they have you, and you're lost!)

A few more tips to keep things rolling:

- Take time a few times a year to sit down with each child and together go through their clothes and toys. Sort out the too-small, the outgrown, and the downtrodden.

- Place bins at bottom of your stairs for each child's clean clothes and collected belongings from all over the house. You won't need to remind them more than 10 times a day to carry the contents of their bin upstairs.

- Get a rubber stamp made with your child's name on it; use it for lunch bags, books, and homework.

- Buy products that don't require an adult to use (my life changed when I started buying tennis shoes that fastened with Velcro).

IF YOU'RE SO INCLINED

I suspect that a lot of toys and equipment get strewn all over children's floors because there is no child-sized table at which to play. Your kids might be more comfortable doing puzzles, games, and building blocks, or coloring and drawing, at their sitting height. If you can spare the room, set up a low table and chairs in your children's rooms or the playroom for these activities.

The absolute key to calmer mornings at your house is organization the night before: lunches at least partially prepared, clothes laid out for quick dressing, permission slips signed, and books packed into backpacks.

■ Use a toy chest for kids' things. If you can't close the lid, do a purge.

■ Make putting clothes away as easy as possible for your children to do themselves: label drawers and shelves. If your kids aren't reading yet, draw simple pictures as labels.

Just try to remember that kids' rooms and playrooms are for kids and play. Try to let go of the magazine shots you envision in your mind as the standard. You can always close the door on the mess, sit down, and read your child a story.

Getting Time on Your Side

	The Old Way	The Lazy Way
Finding a clean pair of matching socks	7 minutes	7 seconds
Locating the "Lion King" puzzle	An hour (and then only half the puzzle pieces)	1 minute (in a plastic bag in the puzzle drawer)
Finding tomorrow's field trip permission slip	45 minutes (all over the house)	5 minutes (in your child's folder)
Sorting the family sock collection	A weekend	30 minutes
Picking up toys	An afternoon	10 minutes

Bringing Your Bathroom to Bear

If you're like most people, you've got too few bathrooms, all of which are too small, with too much stuff in them, shared by too many people with differing standards of neatness and cleanliness. While you're waiting for Tinkerbell to visit and make things right with her magic wand, you can implement some workable solutions to store more and cut the clutter.

THE GREAT CLEAN OUT

The first step to taking control of this room is the great clean out. Not as overwhelming as it sounds, because you can attack one bathroom at a time, and the areas that have to be purged are small—too small. That's why they've got to be streamlined to the max to make use of every inch.

Begin—quickly—by making a major sweep of the countertop, under the sink, all drawers, and around the bathtub and shower ledges. Anywhere you've stashed stuff is the object of

IF YOU'RE SO
INCLINED

A great way to brighten and lighten your bathroom is to install mirrors as large as you have space for. Not only do you gain more primping room, but light is reflected and spaces seem so much larger. Just be careful: If the room gets cluttered again, you'll see double the clutter!

your attention at this point. Whether you have one bathroom or five, the following sections give you steps to follow for each.

What Have You Come Up With? Target Practice

My guess is that you will come up with a small drugstore's supply of beauty supplies, cosmetics, and hair products, dried out in half-empty containers. Use them for target practice and aim for the trash!

Pushing the Envelope: More Purging

Now look at what's left and have another go at tossing things. I know I'm pushing my luck, but try! Will you really ever use that baby sunscreen that you bought when your oldest child was born? Where did all those combs and brushes come from? Can you get rid of most of them? Every bit helps in the throwing-out game. Do what you can.

The White Glove Test

After the great clean out, you're instantly left with more cleared space. You may want to give a quick swipe to clean the areas you just vacated. The space under the sink can get especially dark and mysterious, so pay special attention to it.

You've Done the Hard Part: Now the Fun Part

Now that surfaces are prepared, it's time to group similar things together. Make piles of different items:

- Hair products
- Shaving supplies
- Makeup
- Manicure tools
- First-aid items

They'll all go into a variety of containers, depending on how many you have of any one sort, and how bulky they are. Try the following:

- Baskets—plastic, wicker, or wire
- Covered plastic boxes that stack
- Zip-locking bags
- Plastic turntables

Into the cupboard they go. When you need something, pull out a basket and things will be visible and easy to find.

I use a long, narrow basket meant for holding French bread loaves to hold my makeup. Every morning I pull the basket out of the drawer and place it on the counter. I use what I need and then put the basket back into the drawer when I'm through. All those bottles, tubes, and brushes are in one place, and then can quickly disappear.

Other organizing strategies:

- Buy utensil trays—normally for kitchen use—and put them into paper-lined drawers.

- Keep in the shower stall only those products that are absolutely necessary.

QUICK ⊙ PAINLESS

Another idea for bathroom drawers, which are great collectors of hair and dust, is to line them with terrycloth towels: Things don't slide around and the towels can be easily changed and washed.

- Try a tiny chest of drawers if you can find a spot for it (but don't risk good or antique furniture in the heat and moisture of the bathroom).

- Is there a closet close by the bathroom? Try stealing a little space from it to store extra toilet paper, tissues, shampoo bottles, and toothpaste.

- Have space for a small chair or bench? They can be handy not only as a seat, but also as a table surface. Keeping them clean can be a breeze if you slipcover (or cushion) them in washable terrycloth.

HOW TO FIND SPACE WHERE THERE ISN'T ANY

Need more space? Think up: Floor space is limited, so use the walls whenever possible to squeeze in more storage room.

- Is there room for a shelf or two on any wall in the bathroom? Shelves will hold pretty baskets stashed with supplies.

- Hooks are a great addition; where, besides the standard back of the door, can they be added? Use them for more towels, bathrobes, or a change of clothes.

- The addition of towel racks over existing ones might work for tall people. Or you can install another set of towel racks (or hooks) under existing ones for the short people in your life.

- A wooden rack with three to five pegs can handle towels for a family in the space of a single towel rack.

- Use a caddy made to hang on the shower head to hold bottles and tubes. Edit contents frequently.

- Get a mesh bag to hold kids' bath toys, and hang it over the tub.

- Add storage with the use of a small rolling chest of drawers; makeup, toys, or linens can go into it. Don't forget to consolidate similar things together.

- Scour catalogs for products that fit into your space and increase your storage options: shelf units that use the space over the toilet, corner shelves, towel bars for back of the door, and so on. (Hold Everything has a tremendous selection for bathrooms, Rubbermaid makes a slew of great organizing products, and shop at Target Stores for wonderful organizing items.)

QUICKIE CLEANING: MAINTENANCE MADE EASY

The best improvement you can make to a bathroom is to clean it daily. I'm not talking deep-cleaning here, but enough to keep you from being mortified should a stranger walk in and have to use the facilities. A whisk of the sink, toilet and tank top, a swipe of the counter, and a quick stash of items that belong in drawers will make things presentable.

To make cleanup easier and more likely to happen, keep the cleaning basics under the sink to pull out at a moment's notice.

YOU'LL THANK YOURSELF LATER

If you have a laundry hamper in your bathroom, reevaluate the need for it being there. Perhaps another location, or in each of the bedrooms, could accommodate a hamper and win you back that prized space in the bathroom.

■ I use Clorox™ Clean-Up for just about every surface in the bathroom; it does a great job bleaching anything bleachable (including your clothes if you're not careful!).

■ Spray toilet, tub, and sink as you walk out the door for the day and come back to clean.

■ Keep a toilet brush handy; you can find ones that sit in attractive stands.

■ Your under-the-sink cleaners should also include glass cleaner and scouring powder if you use it. (Don't ever use scouring powder with Clorox Clean-Up, though. You might pass out from the fumes and you'd have an excuse not to clean!)

Keeping up will keep you organized. If you keep things tidy on a daily basis, you'll have to mop the floor and clean the mirrors and glass surfaces only once a week for almost perfection.

KIDS, SAFETY, AND BATHROOMS

Kids have special safety needs in the bathroom. They need a place for everything and need to be able to reach everything they need. Here's how you can help them keep safe and orderly:

■ Put childproof latches on any cupboard that holds cleaning supplies or medications.

■ Remove all glass from the bathroom; it's dangerous and there are so many bright, decorative plastic accessories available to substitute for glass.

Treat yourself to a big, lovely bar of soap (the kind you'd give as a present to someone else), set it on a shelf, and let it scent the bathroom beautifully.

The Lazy Way

- Install anti-slip strips in tub and shower.

- Use bathmats with a non-slip backing.

- Give each bathroom user a drawer, shelf, or basket of his or her own, as well as his or her own hook or peg.

- Give everyone their own plastic glass to hold their toothbrush. Color-code them—everyone gets a different color.

Getting Time On Your Side

	The Old Way	The Lazy Way
Cleaning the bathroom	An afternoon	10 minutes
Finding your makeup/ shaving stuff	5 minutes	2 Seconds
Clearing clutter (with baskets and designated places for stuff)	3 hours, twice a year	3 minutes, three times a week
Changing the towels	10 minutes, mostly looking for matching ones	1 minute
Getting the bathroom ready for company	An afternoon	10 minutes
Cleaning up after the kids	20 minutes (running downstairs for the cleaning supplies)	3 minutes (getting the supplies out of the cabinet under the bathroom sink)

More Lazy Stuff

How to Get Someone Else to Do It

Let's face it. If you liked to organize, you probably would have done it yourself years ago. If you're starting to feel the effects of being disorganized and can't quite catch up by yourself, think about getting help. Life is short, so try to spend most of your time doing things you're good at and that you love to do, and less time on tasks that you're lousy at. One way to accomplish that is by delegating.

DELEGATION: THE HARDEST LESSON

If you're slipping behind, have other priorities, or are filing or cleaning when you could be earning money, it's time to call for help. Anything you delegate is going to require that you—gasp—give up some control. It will never be done exactly the way you've always done it, or in the same sequence or whatever. Let it go, and let someone else assume the responsibility. Of course, you must be clear about your expectations from anyone you hire, and spend the time to go over approximately how you'd like things.

Professional Organizers to the Rescue

You can start by finding help to get you organized. This is where you bring in a professional organizer. Believe it or not, there are people out there who love to organize and can help you—without the emotional turmoil your belongings bring to you—sort through, prioritize, and bring order to your life. Rates vary (from approximately $25 to $125 per hour) as do particular organizers' expertise. But all are excellent at making sense of a home or office. Your investment will be paid back many, many times over.

Where to Find One?

You can find an organizer through the National Association of Professional Organizers, a 10-year-old organization with a national membership of about 1,000 chaos-busters.

Who Needs 'Em?

They are hired by housewives, entrepreneurs, home-based businesses, and huge corporations to make order where there isn't any. They are sensitive to the issues of confidentiality and the sometimes private nature of your business.

Where Can I Get Me One?

You can get a list of professional organizers in your area through NAPO, (512) 206-0151. Or look in your local phone book's Yellow Pages under Organizing Services & Systems-Household & Business. Make calls, get referrals, and go for it!

Here's How

I've worked as a professional organizer with many clients with differing needs, budgets, personalities, and work styles. Regardless of those variables, here's the best way to make the best use of your time with a professional organizer:

- Be sure to get—and call—references beyond the one person who may have given you their name. You want to feel confident that your organizer has a track record.

- Ask the organizer if he or she would give you a free half-hour consultation. That time together will help you determine if you like this person's style and manner—if you have good chemistry.

- Communicate clearly what obstacles you're facing and where you're most behind.

- Never feel embarrassed at your particular situation, be it an office in disarray or toys spread all over the living room. Organizers have seen it all, believe me!

- Listen carefully to the organizer's suggestions. They need your feedback about what sounds reasonable and realistic for you.

- Make a plan together using their expertise in setting up systems in your home or office that will improve your situation. This whole process may take an hour's chat, or your organizer might conduct a formal needs assessment and present a long-term plan to tackle the project.

- You can enlist the organizer to help you through every step of the work. However, if you'd like to cut down billable hours, ask them to leave you a list of "homework" that you need to accomplish by yourself before your next appointment together.

Most often, my clients are so anxious to get organized by the time they've called me that we start working together during our first appointment. Significant transformations often occur in the space of three hours!

Here's When

Sad to say, organizing is an ongoing process, and you have to keep doing it. You'll need to test yourself over a period of time to see if you have the discipline or inclination to keep up the systems you and your organizer created. If not, call the organizer back for "tune-ups" or look at other avenues for help.

Most organizers have varied schedules with each of their clients:

- Every other week

- Once a month (when the mail has stacked up again!)

- Once a quarter

- Once a year

It's up to you to determine how much you can do yourself and how many hours of help you can afford.

MORE HELP OPTIONS!

As for alternatives to professional organizers, here's a long list of suggestions. Think creatively—just because someone is a kid doesn't mean they can't do a better job than you at clearing out the garage.

- You might know of someone who is a "born" organizer. (I'm just sure that people are born carrying the organizing gene or not. If you're reading this book, you probably haven't got it!). Enlist that person's help for an organizing blitz or to come in, say, once a month and keep your papers filed or put the toys back in order.

- Look at your local college as a resource for help; students can be great at clerical tasks at the office or jobs in or outside the house. Most colleges have an employment office—give them a call and discuss your needs.

- You might even get lucky and tie into some kind of internship program at a local college whereby students work for free in exchange for learning some skills.
- Babysitters with a bent for neatness can often do more than just babysit, especially if they're watching older children. Ask if they'd be interested in organizing a child's room or making sense of the junk drawer for extra pay.

Paper Handlers

If you're perpetually behind in your paper work, there are some pros who can help:

- Enlist the help of a bookkeeper—generally a very organized type—to help you get set up and stay current.
- Ask your tax preparer, usually a CPA or Enrolled Agent, to help you get organized or for referrals for those who could help you out.

Keep It Clean

- Getting cleaning help is something you might consider, either a few times a year to get caught up or once a week or more, depending on your budget and need.
- Don't clean for the cleaner, except to put away delicate items or enough clutter so they can do their job most efficiently.
- Another option is to bring in a professional cleaning service once or twice a year to do windows, carpets, and upholstery.

When Mother Nature Needs Taming

If you're on "overwhelm" about your garden, get help. You can choose among several types of services:

- Professional landscaping firms
- Quickie mow n' blow services
- The high school kid across the street
- A combination of all of the above

Just get it done and stop fretting. If your high-maintenance garden is the problem, invest in the services of a garden consultant or landscaper to suggest and implement easy-care changes.

Puppy Love—for Hire

Pets demand love, time, and energy. If they aren't getting the care they need, hire someone to walk them, groom them, play with them, or train them. Leave it to the experts.

GETTING YOUR "LOOK" TOGETHER

If you need to get your clothing in order, must look pulled together every day, don't have a clue how to coordinate your clothes, not sure what you need and couldn't care less, there are experts out there who can help. Here are a few suggestions:

- A few hours of a wardrobe consultant's time could pay big dividends. She will go through your closet with you, help you put together outfits appropriate for your needs and lifestyle, and find the gaps that need filling on your next shopping trip.

- The services of a personal shopper can save you both time and money if you know what you want and what your budget is. Some personal shoppers are affiliated with a department store and know what's in stock and at what price, and can save you endless hours of searching. Usually, their services are free.

- Other personal shoppers are in business for themselves and may offer other services such as color analysis. This type of shopper is not limited to the offerings of just one store and can access a broader range of merchandise and price points.

- Whichever option you choose, your shopper will probably be style-savvy and know local resources. Be sure you are clear about your budget and needs.

- Image consultants, professional organizers, and talented friends or relatives can all do the job if they have fashion sense. It doesn't hurt if they also love to shop!

- Representatives of direct clothing sales organizations such as Doncaster (see Appendix C, "If You Don't Know Where to Get It , Look Here") often act as free advisors, will often go through your closet with you and make a clothing plan.

- Ask the best-dressed women you know if they get help in this area and who they use.

TECHNO CHALLENGES

Your work may demand that you keep up technologically.

- If your computer system is slowing you down, think about a short consultation with a computer consultant to discuss upgrading your system. A pro might help you avoid investing in equipment too sophisticated for your needs, peripherals too powerful for your current system, or an expensive short-term-only fix.

- Tutors are a good way to speed up the learning curve if you're a computer novice. A few hours may save you weeks of plodding frustration.

■ Or hire a tutor to show you the bells and whistles of your software programs so that you can maximize the benefits of your investment.

HELPING KIDS

Children can use tutors, especially if school issues create a less than harmonious atmosphere at your house. Calling in a calm third party could change the dynamics of parent versus child struggles and might make it easier to get through the parts your child is struggling with. (Why do you think there are driving teachers?)

GETTING THE NEST FEATHERED

If your house isn't working, if traffic patterns don't flow, if things look dark or dated but you don't know what to do about it, interview a couple of interior designers to see if they might help you. Sometimes it's so hard to see the answers in your own space. Calling in someone who does this regularly and who has no preconceived notions may supply great solutions.

WORK SPACE SOLUTIONS

At the office, a professional organizer or interior designer with office experience can offer you suggestions to streamline and update your work space.

GET YOURSELF A COACH AND MAKE THE RIGHT MOVES

If you're in business and frantically running from meeting to client or from supplier to customer, and are out of time and energy, you may need help figuring out where you're running to so quickly and why. Take some time out and enlist a business coach. Coaches are a relatively new type of consultant who are trained and can be certified to provide on-going feedback, encouragement and accountability—especially valuable to the self-employed working alone.

Coaches can provide the following services:

- Help you define your work priorities.
- Help you determine what's profitable and what's not, what works, and what you can cut out of your life to keep you on track.
- Some business coaches specialize in money issues and will assist you in looking at your financial picture as well as help you establish a budget.
- Most important, you will have an ongoing relationship with your coach who will check in on you regularly, helping you follow your path to success.

GETTING OUT OF TOWN

If you travel, use travel agents. I know—there are many other choices for making travel arrangements, but if you're short of time, this is one area you can leave to a pro.

THREE SQUARES A DAY

Hate cooking? Consider hiring outside help:

- Have someone come in and cook a few dinners a week by preparing large batches to carry you through several days.
- Use food services that prepare meals—sometimes special heart-healthy cuisine—and deliver them to your door.
- Set up a system with a friend or neighbor: Each of you can prepare double batches and trade one of them.

■ Splurge and pick up an entree from a local restaurant. Add a salad and a piece of fruit for desert, and you've just "cooked" a wonderful meal.

Is meal-planning difficult? Or have you run out of healthy ideas for the kids' lunches? A nutritionist might help. Ask your local hospital, clinic, or doctor's office for referrals. Use the nutritionist to help you make up a healthy menu plan and then stick to it. That way, you don't have to think creatively about this part of your life, and you presumably will have healthy suggestions to follow.

PASSING AROUND THE ODD JOBS

Even small projects that sit semi-permanently on your to-do list can take a toll on your piece of mind, but they are often easy to delegate. Here is a short list of tasks that can often be delegated:

■ Balance the check register

■ Polish all the shoes in the house

■ Purchase plants and baskets in which to place them to decorate the office

■ Errands

■ Prepare a home inventory for insurance purposes

■ Take the car in for servicing

■ Take a load to the dump

■ Start or update your database

■ Do the grocery shopping

■ View, label, and categorize your video tapes

When you can, delegate. The trade-off of peace of mind and efficiency versus budget for steady help, for someone with the aptitude and abilities you lack may be worth it. Just don't trade stress of not getting things done with guilt because they are getting done by others!

If You Really Want More, Read These

Living the Simple Life by Elaine St. James, Hyperion Press, 1996.

Anything by Don Aslett. He's written great books about organizing, throwing out and cleaning, including *Clutter Control, Not For Packrats Only* and *Clutter Free! Finally & Forever*. He also produces a newsletter called the Clean Report; for information call 800-451-2402.

Time Management for Unmanageable People by Ann McGee-Cooper, Bantam Books, 1994.

The Complete Idiot's Guide to Organizing Your Life by Georgene Lockwood, Alpha Books, 1996.

Taming the Paper Tiger: Organizing the Paper in Your Life by Barbara Hemphill, Kiplinger Books, 1992.

Getting Organized by Stephanie Winston, Warner Books, 1991.

How to Conquer Clutter by Stephanie Culp, Writer's Digest Books, 1989.

Clean Your House The Lazy Way by Barbara H. Durham, Alpha Books, 1998.

Organizing Options; Solutions from Professional Organizers compiled by the San Francisco Bay Area Chapter of the National Association of Professional Organizers, 1994. Available from SFBA NAPO, 1952 Union Street #721, San Francisco CA 94123.

Two great books by Connie Cox and Cris Evatt; *Simply Organized!: The Practical Way to Simplify Your Complicated Life*, Berkley Publishing Group, 1991; and *30 Days to a Simpler Life*, Plume Publishing, 1998. The first book covers a myriad of wonderful tips to get you organized. *A Simpler Life* goes beyond organization to a concept that can have an even more profound impact on your life.

The Seven Habits of Highly Effective People; Powerful Lessons in Personal Change by Stephen R. Covey, A Simon & Schuster Fireside book, 1990.

Kitchen Organization Tips & Secrets, by Deniece Schofield, Bettweway Publications, 1996. Everything you'd like to know abut organizing kitchen space and kitchen work, improving work flow and meal planning ideas.

Totally Organized by Bonnie McCullogh, St. Martin's Press, 1989, covers home and family issues.

Organized to be the Best! by Susan Silver, Adams-Hall Publishing, 1995. A good guide to work and office organizational challenges, including office set up, using the computer and business travel tips.

If You Don't Know Where to Get It, Look Here

GENERAL ORGANIZING PRODUCTS & SERVICES

Stores

Ordning & Reda, a Swedish company. Beautifully designed line of stationery, notebooks, photo albums, pens and pencils. Has a Manhattan location. 212/799-0828.

Target; nationwide.

Hold Everything stores and catalog. Everything to store anything you can name: clothing, books, CDs, kitchen gear, sports, and play stuff. 800/421-2264.

Racor. Has great racks for outdoor equipment. 800/783-7725.

Catalogs

Reliable Home Office. Home office needs from furniture to phones to pens. 800/869-6000.

The Benefiicary Book. Published by Active Insights. 800/222-9125; www. benebook@aol.com.

The Container Store. Swedish Elfa wire basket shelf, drawer and accessory system for closets. Wonderful kitchen and pantry products: stacking baskets, shelf systems, pantry shelving components. These products can be used in offices, kids' rooms, and bathrooms. Stores nationwide or order from catalog. 800/733-3532.

Get Organized. General organizing aids, including good kitchen items. 800/803-9400; getorginc.com.

Lillian Vernon. Offers an organizing products catalog called "Neat Ideas for an Organized Life." 800/285-5555.

Solutions. This catalog sells a wide variety of household organizing tools, including the Space Bag Storage System (Item #62515). 800/342-9988.

Lizell. Office supplies from furniture to pens. 800/718-8808; www.lizell.com.

Techline. A line of high-quality laminated furniture components that can be used in anywhere one needs attractive storage. Call their Wisconsin factory to find a showroom or retail outlet near you. 608/849-4181.

OFFICE SUPPLIES

Stores

Staples, Office Depot, and **Office Max.**

Catalogs

Abbot Office Systems. Stackable drawers and cubbies to organize paper, mail, and supplies at the office or in your home. 800/631-2233.

Hello Direct. Every imaginable telephone, telephone and teleconferencing system, and telephone headsets to meet just about any need. 800/444-3556; hello-direct.com.

Quill. Quickly ships the full spectrum of office supplies at great prices. 800/789-1331; quillcorp.com.

Fox Bay Industries. Offers quality ergonomic merchandise: keyboard wrist supports, chairs, footrests, and other office products, most with a five-year limited warranty. 800/874-8527.

Levenger *Tools for Serious Readers,* including writing instruments, desk accessories, paper products, and a great system of notebooks and calendars called "Circa." 800/544-0880; www.levenger.com.

Exposures. Organizing products for photographs; albums, frames, boxes, and cabinets. 800/222-4947.

Anthro Corporation, Technology furniture. Desks that not only glide around on wheels, but can easily be raised up or down for those who like to work standing up; carts that hold a computer monitor in a tilted position for viewing comfort. Interesting products. 800/325-3841; www.anthro.com.

Light Impressions. Archival supplies for photographs, slides and negatives, plus some general storage solutions. 800/828-6216.

Rosemount Office Systems. Flexible office space systems. 800/328-6446.

The Mobile Office Outfitter. Great products for your car, van, or truck, such as mobile workstations that strap into your passenger seat, mobile phone holders, and organizers that fit into your trunk. 800/426-3453; www.mobilegear.com.

Stationery

Quill. Everyday business items. 800/789-1331; quillcorp.com.

Tiffany & Co. 800/526-0649.

Levenger *Tools for Serious Readers.* Offers Crane & Company products. 800/544-0880.

American Stationery Co, Inc. 800/822-2577.

Bins

Rubbermaid. Bins, boxes, storage containers, stackable drawers, and baskets in many sizes. Available nationwide. Write for a home products or industrial products catalog: Rubbermaid Inc.; Home Products Division; 1147 Akron Road; Wooster, OH 44691-6000. 800/362-1000.

Labelling

Brother Labeling System. Toll free 1-877-4PTOUCH; brother.com.

Kroy Labelers. 800/733-5769.

Rubber Stamps

XStamper. Every imaginable kind of custom rubber stamp. 800/851-2686; www.xstamper.com.

TIME MANAGEMENT

Day-Timer. Personal organizers, both in paper and software. Good quality and flexible systems. 800/225-5005; www.daytimer.com.

DayRunner. Great organizers and organizing products. Order their catalog from DayRunner Direct, 800/643-9923; dayrunner.com.

At-A-Glance. This company manufactures several complete lines of planners, appointment books and calendars in every conceivable format. You can create your own personalized datebook system choosing among the many forms and accessories At-A-Glance offers, from blank sheets, to expense forms to contact records. Then consolidate them in a choice of binders. At-A-Glance also offers some useful fun: Dilbert, Mickey Mouse and Winnie The Pooh calendars and planners. Available at many office supply stores or 800/333-1125; www.at-a-glance.com.

Filofax systems. Can be purchased from Charals online at www.direct.ca/charals/filo.htm.

TimeWise. This company makes a line of display boards with a shiny white surface that you can wipe clean—for organization, communication, and planning purposes. You can find 3- to 12-month calendar boards, different configurations to display information and boards to track projects. 800/523-8060.

FOOD

Horizon Foods. 888/EASYFOOD; www.horizonfood.com.

Net Grocer. www.netgrocer.com

Matol Botanical International. Sells the great little portable battery-operated shaker mixer, item # 07649-000. 800/363-6890; FAX 800/363-8890; www.info@matol.com.

CLOTHING

Doncaster. Fine-quality, classic women's clothing that you can purchase in an hour from a personal consultant. Call 800/669-3662 to find a consultant near you, or log on to www.doncaster.com.

TOTES

Lands End. 800/356-4444.

L. L. Bean. 800/221-4221.

Walker. These mesh bags can be found at Ad Hoc Softwares in NYC, 212/925-2652. I've also seen them in department stores and art supply stores.

Le Sportsac. Found in department stores. 800/486-2247 or 212/736-6262.

AmeriBag. Can be ordered through TravelSmith. 800/950-1600.

TRAVEL

Orvis Travel catalog. From clothing to converters to clocks. 800/541-3541.

TravelSmith. Luggage and great-looking go-anywhere travel clothes for both men and women. Their customer service people will even help you plan a travel wardrobe. Call 800/950-1600 for catalog.

CLOSET/STORAGE BUILDERS

Closet Connection (in SF Bay Area). 800/499-7766.

California Closets. 800/274-6754.

Poliform. Top-of-the-line closet designs using the finest woods, glass, wood and metal doors, custom lighting, and pull-down bars and racks. 212/421-1220

The Great American Closet Company. 800/305-8555.

RECYCLING

Goodwill Industries. 800/664-6577.

LensCrafters. Has a "Give the Gift of Sight" program which distributes used eyeglasses to needy people all over the world. Call 800/522-LENS for the nearest LensCrafters location.

Nike. Will take your old athletic shoes as part of their "Reuse-A-Shoe" program. They're made into athletic equipment such as playground padding. Call 800/352-NIKE for a drop-off location near you.

MiraMed Institute. Accepts donations of still-good prescription and over-the-counter-medicines and sends them to Russian orphans. 800/441-1917.

GreenDisk. An organization that recycles used computer discs and CD-ROMs into new products. Send discs to CDIP Program; 5640 S. Durango; Tacoma, WA 98409; or call 800/305-DISK.

Used computers are probably welcome at your local school, church, or non-profit organization.

ECO Media recycles your old video tapes; 5429 La Palma Avenue; Anaheim Hills, CA 92807. 800/359-4601.

HEALTH CARE

CraKel Publications. Personal Health-Care Organizer. 800/708-7623; www.andreas.com/crakel.

ELECTRONIC ORGANIZERS:

3Com. PalmPilots. 800/881-7256; www.palm.com.

PICTURES AND PHOTOS

Creative Memories. 888/227-6748.

It's Time for Your Reward

Once You've Done This:	Reward Yourself:
Written down your top 20 dinner menus	Go out to dinner
Cleaned under the bathroom sink	Book a massage
Donated all but three sweatshirts	Buy that framed print you've been lusting after
Thrown out half your magazines	Spend the afternoon reading at the library
Caught up with your filing	Buy yourself a beautiful plant for your office
Cleared off your dresser in your bedroom	Leave the office half an hour early
Prepared a chart of household chores	Adopt a pet from the animal shelter
Made the LPs go away	Buy yourself a new CD
Put up shelves in the garage	Go to a movie
Recycled all your old computer manuals	Order that cool mousepad

Index

Now you can do these tasks, too!

The Lazy Way

Starting to think there are a few more of life's little tasks that you've been putting off? Don't worry—we've got you covered. Take a look at all of *The Lazy Way* books available. Just imagine—you can do almost anything *The Lazy Way!*

Clean Your House The Lazy Way
By Barbara H. Durham
0-02-862649-4

Handle Your Money The Lazy Way
By Sarah Young Fisher and Carol Turkington
0-02-862632-X

Care for Your Home The Lazy Way
By Terry Meany
0-02-862646-X

Train Your Dog The Lazy Way
By Andrea Arden
0-87605180-8

Take Care of Your Car The Lazy Way
By Michael Kennedy and Carol Turkington
0-02-862647-8

Keep Your Kids Busy The Lazy Way
By Barbara Nielsen and Patrick Wallace
0-02-863013-0

*All Lazy Way books are just $12.95!

additional titles on the back!

Build Your Financial Future The Lazy Way

By Terry Meany

0-02-862648-6

Shed Some Pounds The Lazy Way

By Annette Cain and Becky Cortopassi-Carlson

0-02-862999-X

Cook Your Meals The Lazy Way

By Sharon Bowers

0-02-862644-3

Feed Your Kids Right The Lazy Way

By Virginia Van Vynckt

0-02-863001-7

Cut Your Spending The Lazy Way

By Leslie Haggin

0-02-863002-5

Stop Aging The Lazy Way

By Judy Myers, Ph.D.

0-02-862793-8

Get in Shape The Lazy Way

By Annette Cain

0-02-863010-6

Learn French The Lazy Way

By Christophe Desmaison

0-02-863011-4

Learn Italian The Lazy Way

By Gabrielle Euvino

0-02-863014-9

Learn Spanish The Lazy Way

By Steven Hawson

0-02-862650-8